MW01493038

ACADEMIC SKILLS PROBLEMS
FIFTH EDITION WORKBOOK

ACADEMIC SKILLS PROBLEMS
Fifth Edition Workbook

Edward S. Shapiro
Nathan H. Clemens

THE GUILFORD PRESS
New York   London

Copyright © 2023 The Guilford Press
A Division of Guilford Publications, Inc.
370 Seventh Avenue, Suite 1200, New York, NY 10001
www.guilford.com

All rights reserved

Except as indicated, no part of this book may be reproduced, translated, stored in a
retrieval system, or transmitted, in any form or by any means, electronic, mechanical,
photocopying, microfilming, recording, or otherwise, without written permission from
the publisher.

Printed in the United States of America

This book is printed on acid-free paper.

Last digit is print number: 9   8   7   6   5   4   3   2   1

LIMITED DUPLICATION LICENSE

These materials are intended for use only by qualified professionals.

The publisher grants to individual purchasers of this book nonassignable permission
to reproduce all materials for which photocopying permission is specifically granted in
a footnote. This license is limited to you, the individual purchaser, for personal use or
use with students. This license does not grant the right to reproduce these materials for
resale, redistribution, electronic display, or any other purposes (including but not limited
to books, pamphlets, articles, video or audio recordings, blogs, file-sharing sites, Internet
or intranet sites, and handouts or slides for lectures, workshops, or webinars, whether
or not a fee is charged). Permission to reproduce these materials for these and any other
purposes must be obtained in writing from the Permissions Department of Guilford
Publications.

The authors have checked with sources believed to be reliable in their efforts to provide
information that is complete and generally in accord with the standards of practice that
are accepted at the time of publication. However, in view of the possibility of human error
or changes in behavioral, mental health, or medical sciences, neither the authors, nor the
editor and publisher, nor any other party who has been involved in the preparation or
publication of this work warrants that the information contained herein is in every respect
accurate or complete, and they are not responsible for any errors or omissions or the
results obtained from the use of such information. Readers are encouraged to confirm the
information contained in this book with other sources.

ISBN 978-1-4625-5138-5

About the Authors

Edward S. Shapiro, PhD, until his death in 2016, was Director of the Center for Promoting Research to Practice and Professor in the School Psychology Program at Lehigh University. Best known for his work in curriculum-based assessment and nonstandardized methods of assessing academic skills problems, Dr. Shapiro was the author or coauthor of numerous books and other publications, and presented papers, chaired symposia, and delivered invited addresses at conferences around the world. Dr. Shapiro's contributions to the field of school psychology have been recognized with the Outstanding Contributions to Training Award from Trainers of School Psychologists, the Distinguished Contribution to School Psychology Award from the Pennsylvania Psychological Association, the Eleanor and Joseph Lipsch Research Award from Lehigh University, and the Senior Scientist Award from the Division of School Psychology of the American Psychological Association, among other honors.

Nathan H. Clemens, PhD, is Professor in the Department of Special Education and Dean's Distinguished Faculty Fellow at The University of Texas at Austin. He is a member of the Board of Directors of the Meadows Center for Preventing Educational Risk. Dr. Clemens's research is focused on intervention and assessment for students with learning difficulties, with an emphasis on word reading difficulties among students in early elementary grades and reading comprehension difficulties for students in secondary grades. He has published over 60 peer-reviewed journal articles and chapters in edited books and is leading several federally funded research projects investigating interventions for academic skills. Dr. Clemens is a recipient of the Outstanding Dissertation Award and the Lightner Witmer Award for Early Career Scholarship from the Division of School Psychology of the American Psychological Association.

Contents

Purchasers of this book can download and print the reproducible
forms at *www.guilford.com/shapiro2-forms* for personal use or use with
students (see copyright page for details).

List of Forms

Introduction

The purpose of this workbook is to provide forms, instructions, and other materials to supplement *Academic Skills Problems, Fifth Edition: Direct Assessment and Intervention*. The workbook offers elaboration and detail of material covered in the text and also provides additional forms to supplement those in the text. Some forms in the text are duplicated in the workbook for ease in copying; users of the manual are granted permission from the publisher to copy and modify these forms for their personal use. Although the workbook can certainly be used on its own, its purpose is to complement, rather than stand independent from, the text.

The workbook also offers opportunities for learning, practicing, and mastering many of the skills discussed in the text. For example, a complete manual related to the use of the Behavioral Observation of Students in Schools (BOSS) and BOSS Modified observation codes are provided. Full definitions of the BOSS and BOSS Modified behavioral categories, as well as instructions for collecting information, scoring the observations, and interpreting the data, are given. Also included are forms for completing teacher and student interviews, along with a useful checklist for obtaining teacher reports for academic behavior.

With the continued implementation of multi-tiered systems of support (MTSS) as a framework for delivering needed services to all students, especially at the elementary level, resources are provided that support the processes of assessment and data-based decision making. In particular, forms useful for organizing data from universal screening and from progress monitoring, and forms that document team decision making related to instructional decisions, are all provided.

In the area of conducting the direct assessment of academic skills, the workbook offers additional instructions and practice exercises in the assessment process. In particular, detailed explanations of using such measures as *digits correct per minute* and *correct letter sequences* to score math and spelling are provided. The workbook also offers a description of and exercises in how to graph data, make data-based decisions, collect local norms, and other tasks related to a direct assessment of academic skills.

1

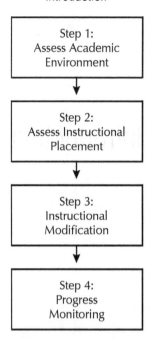

FIGURE 1. Integrated model of curriculum-based assessment. Adapted from Shapiro (1990, p. 334). Copyright © National Association of School Psychologists, Inc. Reprinted by permission of Taylor & Francis Ltd, *http://www.tandfonline.com* on behalf of National Association of School Psychologists, Inc.

The workbook follows the model of assessment described in the *Academic Skills Problems* text and depicted in Figure 1. The first section, corresponding to Step 1 of the assessment process—assessing the academic environment (see Figure 2)—provides materials for interviewing teachers and students, conducting direct observations, and using informant report data (a teacher rating scale). The next section, corresponding to Step 2 of the process—directly assessing instructional placement—provides information related to the processes involved in the direct

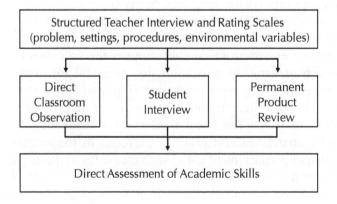

FIGURE 2. Flowchart of procedures for assessing academic skills.

assessment of academic skills (in particular, details about the assessment of reading, math, spelling, and written language). This section contains information on both the use of short- and long-term data collection procedures.

The next section of the workbook, corresponding to Step 3 of the process, offers details on the use of two powerful instructional interventions: the *incremental rehearsal* technique and *cover–copy–compare*. The fourth section, corresponding to Step 4—progress monitoring—provides additional examples on the graphic display of data, offers practice in making different kinds of decisions based on progress monitoring data, and explains how to collect local norms that can be used for goal setting. This final section offers materials for supporting MTSS implementation and response-to-intervention decisions, with particular attention to data-based decision-making components.

Throughout, readers will find detailed "how to" explanations offered in a step-by-step fashion. Practice exercises are also provided, and readers are encouraged to develop their own exercises modeled on those in the workbook.

Assessing the Academic Environment

Teacher Interview

The assessment process begins with the teacher interview. Several forms are provided to facilitate the interview. The Teacher Interview Form (Form 1), which is also printed in *Academic Skills Problems, Fifth Edition*, suggests the specific questions and domains that should be addressed for each academic area when interviewing teachers. It is designed to be completed during a face-to-face meeting with a teacher. The key objectives of the interview are to gather information on the nature and extent of the student's academic difficulties, which will help the evaluator focus subsequent assessment activities, and to understand the interventions that have already been tried or are currently in place. In addition, understanding the "big picture" of skill development in reading, mathematics, and writing is helpful for fully understanding the student's problem from the teacher's perspective. Across academic areas, the form provides a basis for better understanding the nature and scope of the student's difficulties. Form 2, which provides a list of elementary math computational objectives, can be used with Form 1 for students with mathematics difficulties.

Given the significant presence of MTSS models in schools, it is important to understand the nature of the model, how specific components of the model are structured by the school, the nature of the assessment processes in place, and the way in which data-based decision making is conducted. The Teacher Interview Form (Form 1) asks for this information. Some teachers may not be the best source of all this information. It is suggested that users of the interview form consider asking for this information from relevant school personnel (e.g., principals, instructional specialists, school psychologists, lead teachers). The inclusion of a section of the interview form devoted to MTSS is provided for academic skills, with an additional question regarding whether a model for behavior is in place.

Readers are reminded that the teacher interview is the starting point of an academic assessment and is not intended to be an exhaustive source of information. Users of the Teacher Interview Form are encouraged to omit questions that the teacher already addressed or skip sections that are not relevant to the referred student. The teacher interview should be brief (ideally, under 15 minutes) to respect the teacher's time. The most valuable information for understanding the student's academic difficulties and what to do about them will come through the direct assessment and intervention activities in subsequent steps. The teacher interview helps the evaluator determine the next steps in the assessment process, such as when to observe the student and what academic skills to assess directly. Any additional information needed from the teacher can be obtained after the interview.

Interviews with teachers should also obtain general information about how they manage instruction and the classroom environment as well as the nature of the strategies already attempted to remediate the problem behavior of the student. Included in the interview is information about the success or failure of these strategies. In addition to, or instead of using The Teacher Interview Form, some evaluators may prefer to be guided by more general questions, which are provided in Form 3. This format specifically asks questions around instructional practices, curriculum, assessment, and management. Typically, the interview is conducted following an observation of the teacher teaching the student of interest. The questions in Form 3 are useful to guide this type of interview that follows a direct observation.

Teacher Interview Form for Identification of Academic Difficulties

Student_____   Teacher_____

School _____   Grade _____   Interviewer _____

Date of interview _____

Suggested introductory language:

The purpose of this interview is to gather some basic information on [student's] areas of academic difficulty and functioning in the classroom. This information will be highly useful in guiding my assessment. Some of the questions will involve the academic curricula, materials, and instructional groupings or routines that you use. These questions are meant to better understand the student's difficulties in the current context, and are not meant to evaluate any aspects of your teaching.

1. General Information and Referral Concerns

What is primary academic area of concern (reading, math, or written expression)? _____

_____

Are there any additional areas of difficulty (reading, math, or written expression)? _____

_____

Areas of relative strength for the student (i.e., skill areas that are strongest for this student specifically):

_____

_____

2. Primary Area of Concern

2A. What specific aspects of [primary area of difficulty—reading, math, or written expression] are problematic? _____

_____

2B. Intervention and Support Strategies

Have they received any supplementary support or intervention in this area? _____

_____

What kind of strategies have been tried, and to what extent were they successful? _____

_____

_____

2C. Curriculum and Instruction in Area of Primary Concern

Title of curriculum or series used in this area_____

Are there other instructional materials used in addition or in place of the curriculum? _____

_____

(continued)

From *Academic Skills Problems Fifth Edition Workbook* by Edward S. Shapiro and Nathan H. Clemens. Copyright © 2023 The Guilford Press. Permission to photocopy this form is granted to purchasers of this book for personal use or use with students (see copyright page for details). Purchasers can download additional copies of this form (see the box at the end of the table of contents).

At this point in the school year, what types of skills are students expected to demonstrate in this area? _____

_____

_____

What time do you typically teach this subject? _____

3. Secondary Area of Concern *(if applicable)*

3A. What specific aspects of [secondary area of difficulty—reading, math, or writing] are problematic? _____

_____

_____

3B. Intervention and Support Strategies

Have they received any supplementary support or intervention in this area? _____

_____

What kind of strategies have been tried, and to what extent were they successful? _____

_____

_____

3C. Curriculum and Instruction in Secondary Area of Concern

Title of curriculum or series_____

Are there other instructional materials used in addition or in place of the curriculum? _____

_____

At this point in the school year, what skills are students expected to demonstrate in this area? _____

_____

_____

_____

What time do you typically teach this subject? _____

4. Behavior

Next I'd like to ask about [student's] behavior and learning-related skills during academic instruction and activities. On a scale of 0 to 5, with 0 being "never" and 5 being "always," please indicate how often the student demonstrates the behavior during academic instruction and activities.

	Never			Always	
a. Stays engaged (on-task) during teacher-led large group instruction	1	2	3	4	5
b. Stays engaged (on-task) during teacher-led small group instruction	1	2	3	4	5
c. Stays engaged (on-task) during partner work or independent work	1	2	3	4	5
d. Follows directions	1	2	3	4	5
e. Shows effort and persistence, even when work is difficult	1	2	3	4	5
f. Asks for help when needed	1	2	3	4	5
g. Completes tests or classwork in allotted time	1	2	3	4	5
h. Completes homework on time	1	2	3	4	5
i. Engages in behaviors that disrupt instruction or peers' learning	1	2	3	4	5

(continued)

Is [student's] behavior especially problematic in some academic subjects or activities than others?

_____

_____

Additional information on the student's behavior or social skills that either facilitate or interfere with their learning or the classroom environment (follow up on items rated as problematic above) _____

_____

_____

_____

_____

5. Reading

This space is available to note if the student demonstrates difficulties in reading. *If there are no indicated problems with reading, this section should be skipped.*

Next I'd like to ask about [student's] skills in some specific areas related to reading, and whether they are below expectations, meeting expectations, or above expectations in each area at this time of the year.

Phonological and Phonemic Awareness: Able to identify sounds in words, rhyme, blend, segment, etc.	
Alphabet Knowledge and Letter Recognition: Able to identify printed letters, able to correctly associate printed letters (and letter combinations) with sounds	
Word Reading/Decoding: Reads words accurately; able to decode (i.e., sound out) unfamiliar words; reads grade-appropriate words with ease and automaticity	
Reading Fluency: Able to read text smoothly, accurately, with expression	
Reading Comprehension: Understands what is read; able to answer both literal and inferential questions from a passage; comprehends both narrative and expository texts	
Vocabulary: Has age-appropriate knowledge of word meanings and definitions	

If Word Reading/Decoding skills are a concern, what types of words does the student find challenging? _____

What types of words is the student more successful at reading? _____

How would you describe this student's listening (oral) comprehension skills—can they understand your directions, and understand stories or answer questions correctly after listening? _____

_____

How is instructional time in reading typically divided between large group instruction, small group instruction, and partner or independent work? _____

_____

_____

(continued)

11

Does this student also have difficulty with spelling? _____

_____

6. Mathematics

This space is available to note if the student demonstrates difficulties with specific mathematics skill areas. If there are no previously indicated problems with mathematics, this section should be skipped.

Next I'd like to ask about [student's] skills in some specific areas related to math, and whether they are below expectations, meeting expectations, or above expectations in each area at this time of the year.

Early Numerical Competencies (Number Sense, Early Numeracy): Age/grade-appropriate skills and understanding in ***counting***, number recognition, quantity discrimination, cardinality	
Addition and Subtraction Math Facts: Grade-appropriate accuracy and fluency with addition and subtraction math facts within 20	
Multidigit Addition and Subtraction Operations: Grade-appropriate skills in applying procedures/algorithms for accurately solving addition and subtraction problems	
Multiplication and Division Math Facts: Grade-appropriate accuracy and fluency with multiplication and division math facts within 100	
Multidigit Multiplication and Division Operations: Grade-appropriate skills in applying procedures/algorithms for accurately solving multiplication and division problems	
Fractions, Decimals, Percent: Grade-appropriate understanding and skills in rational numbers including comparing magnitude, accurately completing operations, converting, etc.	
Word Problem Solving Skills: Able to solve grade-appropriate word problems	
Geometry and Measurement: Conceptual knowledge and ability to solve grade-appropriate geometry and measurement problems	
Pre-Algebra and Algebra: Conceptual knowledge and ability to solve grade-appropriate pre-algebra and algebra operations	

How is instructional time in math typically divided between large group instruction, small group instruction, and partner or independent work? _____

_____

_____

(continued)

7. Writing

This space is available to note if the student demonstrates difficulties with specific writing skill areas (Note: if a student has reading difficulties, it is very possible they have difficulties in writing as well).

Next I'd like to ask about [student's] skills in some specific areas related to writing, and whether they are above expectations, below expectations, or meeting expectations in this area at this time of the year.

Handwriting	
Typing/Keyboarding (if applicable)	
Spelling	
Capitalization and/or punctuation	
Grammar and syntax	
Planning and Formulating Ideas Before Writing	
Organization and Coherence	
Story/passage length	
Editing and Revising	

What types of writing assignments are given at this time of year, and what types of skills are students expected to demonstrate? _____

_____

_____

Does the student have difficulty with low motivation to write, and/or self-regulation skills that affect their writing output and quality? _____

_____

_____

8. School MTSS/RTI Model

Information on the schoolwide multi-tiered system of support (MTSS) or response to intervention (RTI) model in academics and/or behavior, if one exists, can be obtained below. For efficiency, this information might be better obtained outside of the teacher interview.

What does the model look like: Grade levels covered, skill areas targeted, etc. _____

_____

_____

What Tier 2 interventions are available? _____

_____

_____

Is there a Tier 3, and what does that entail? _____

_____

_____

How are students identified for Tier 2 or Tier 3 interventions (e.g., universal screening)? _____

_____

(continued)

How often is progress monitored for students receiving Tier 2 or Tier 3 interventions, and what measure(s) are used? _____

_____

What and who determines when students move between tiers or interventions are adjusted? _____

_____

9. Preliminary Hypothesis Formation (to be completed after the interview)

Primary area of difficulty: _____

Suspected skill deficits that are the reason for the difficulty: _____

_____

Difficulties with behaviors or learning-related skills that may be contributing to the problem: _____

_____

Possible environmental and instructional factors contributing to the problem: _____

_____

Relative strengths (academic or social/behavioral) that may mitigate the problem: _____

_____

Preliminary Hypothesis Statement Framework. This is meant as a guide to assist hypothesis writing. It will be refined and revised across the subsequent assessment. Separate hypotheses can be written for secondary areas of difficulty.

_____'s difficulties in [reading/mathematics/writing] are due to inadequate or underdeveloped skills in _____. These difficulties appear [or do not appear] to be related to the student's behaviors or learning-related skills, which may include _____ _____. The student's difficulties appear [or do not appear] to be related to instructional or classroom environment factors, which may include _____. Compared to their area(s) of difficulty, the student demonstrates relative strengths in _____ _____.

_____'s difficulties in [reading/mathematics/writing] are due to inadequate or underdeveloped skills in _____. These difficulties appear [or do not appear] to be related to the student's behaviors or learning-related skills, which may include _____ _____. The student's difficulties appear [or do not appear] to be related to instructional or classroom environment factors, which may include _____. Compared to their area(s) of difficulty, the student demonstrates relative strengths in _____ _____.

_____'s difficulties in [reading/mathematics/writing] are due to inadequate or underdeveloped skills in _____. These difficulties appear [or do not appear] to be related to the student's behaviors or learning-related skills, which may include _____ _____. The student's difficulties appear [or do not appear] to be related to instructional or classroom environment factors, which may include _____. Compared to their area(s) of difficulty, the student demonstrates relative strengths in _____ _____.

A Computation Skills Mastery Curriculum

GRADE 1

1. Add two one-digit numbers: sums to 10
2. Subtract two one-digit numbers: combinations to 10

GRADE 2

3. Add two one-digit numbers: sums 11–19
4. Add a one-digit number to a two-digit number—no regrouping
5. Add a two-digit number to a two-digit number—no regrouping
6. Add a three-digit number to a three-digit number—no regrouping
7. Subtract a one-digit number from a one- or two-digit number—combinations to 18
8. Subtract a one-digit number from a two-digit number—no regrouping
9. Subtract a two-digit number from a two-digit number—no regrouping
10. Subtract a three-digit number from a three-digit number—no regrouping
11. Multiplication facts—0's, 1's, 2's

GRADE 3

12. Add three or more one-digit numbers
13. Add three or more two-digit numbers—no regrouping
14. Add three or more three- and four-digit numbers—no regrouping
15. Add a one-digit number to a two-digit number with regrouping
16. Add a two-digit number to a two-digit number with regrouping
17. Add a two-digit number to a three-digit number with regrouping from the 10's column only
18. Add a two-digit number to a three-digit number with regrouping from the 100's column only
19. Add a two-digit number to a three-digit number with regrouping from 10's and 100's columns
20. Add a three-digit number to a three-digit number with regrouping from the 10's column only
21. Add a three-digit number to a three-digit number with regrouping from the 100's column only
22. Add a three-digit number to a three-digit number with regrouping from the 10's and 100's columns
23. Add a four-digit number to a four-digit number with regrouping in one to three columns
24. Subtract two four-digit numbers—no regrouping
25. Subtract a one-digit number from a two-digit number with regrouping
26. Subtract a two-digit number from a two-digit number with regrouping
27. Subtract a two-digit number from a three-digit number with regrouping from the 10's column only
28. Subtract a two-digit number from a three-digit number with regrouping from the 100's column only
29. Subtract a two-digit number from a three-digit number with regrouping from the 10's and 100's columns
30. Subtract a three-digit number from a three-digit number with regrouping from the 10's column only

(continued)

From *Academic Skills Problems Fifth Edition Workbook* by Edward S. Shapiro and Nathan H. Clemens. Copyright © 2023 The Guilford Press. Permission to photocopy this form is granted to purchasers of this book for personal use or use with students (see copyright page for details). Purchasers can download additional copies of this form (see the box at the end of the table of contents).

31. Subtract a three-digit number from a three-digit number with regrouping from the 100's column only
32. Subtract a three-digit number from a three-digit number with regrouping from the 10's and 100's columns
33. Multiplication facts—3–9

GRADE 4

34. Add a five- or six-digit number to a five- or six-digit number with regrouping in any column
35. Add three or more two-digit numbers with regrouping
36. Add three or more three-digit numbers with regrouping
37. Subtract a five- or six-digit number from a five- or six-digit number with regrouping in any column
38. Multiply a two-digit number by a one-digit number with no regrouping
39. Multiply a three-digit number by a one-digit number with no regrouping
40. Multiply a two-digit number by a one-digit number with no regrouping
41. Multiply a three-digit number by a one-digit number with regrouping
42. Division facts—0–9
43. Divide a two-digit number by a one-digit number with no remainder
44. Divide a two-digit number by a one-digit number with remainder
45. Divide a three-digit number by a one-digit number with remainder
46. Divide a four-digit number by a one-digit number with remainder

GRADE 5

47. Multiply a two-digit number by a two-digit number with regrouping
48. Multiply a three-digit number by a two-digit number with regrouping
49. Multiply a three-digit number by a three-digit number with regrouping

Questions to Guide General Teacher Interviews
for Academic Skills

Teacher _____   Student _____

Academic subject(s) _____   Date _____

1. What was the specific instructional assignment being taught during the observation?

2. How was the instructional assignment presented to the student?

3. What opportunities were presented for guided practice?

4. What opportunities were presented for independent practice?

5. What opportunities were presented for feedback to students?

6. What were the specific objectives of the instructional lesson observed?

7. How did you determine whether the student was successful during the lesson observed?

8. What type of additional support beyond your normal classroom instruction does this student need to succeed?

9. What strategies seem to work with this student?

10. What strategies do not seem to work with this student?

11. What types of assessment information do you collect?

12. How do you use the information gathered about student performance?

13. During group instruction, what clues do you use to evaluate a student's performance?

14. What adaptations do you make or permit on assignments?

15. What adaptations do you make or permit on tests?

16. What kind of support can you expect from supervisors and administrators for more intensive intervention changes if they are needed?

Many thanks to Christine Schubel, EdS, for her contributions to this form.

From *Academic Skills Problems Fifth Edition Workbook* by Edward S. Shapiro and Nathan H. Clemens. Copyright © 2023 The Guilford Press. Permission to photocopy this form is granted to purchasers of this book for personal use or use with students (see copyright page for details). Purchasers can download additional copies of this form (see the box at the end of the table of contents).

Student Interview

It can be helpful in the process of academic assessment to determine how the student perceives the demands of the academic environment, and their perceptions of their academic performance. This information is best obtained through an interview of the student. Specifically, questions should cover the following areas: the degree to which the student understands directions of assignments; the degree of success predicted by the student on each assignment; the student's perception of how much time they are given by the teacher to complete assignments; the student's knowledge of how to seek assistance when experiencing difficulty; and the student's understanding of the consequences of not completing academic work. This information can be obtained by means of a semistructured interview, conducted immediately after an observation of the student engaged in an assigned task. A simple format with general guidelines is provided for conducting the interview (Form 4).

Student Interview Form

Student name _____

Subject _____

Date _____

STUDENT-REPORTED BEHAVIOR

_____ None completed for this area

Understands expectations of teacher	☐ Yes	☐ No	☐ Not sure
Understands assignments	☐ Yes	☐ No	☐ Not sure
Feels they can do the assignments	☐ Yes	☐ No	☐ Not sure
Likes the subject	☐ Yes	☐ No	☐ Not sure
Feels they are given enough time to complete assignments	☐ Yes	☐ No	☐ Not sure
Feels like they are called on to participate in discussions	☐ Yes	☐ No	☐ Not sure
Feels like they can improve in [referred skill area] with effort and support	☐ Yes	☐ No	☐ Not sure

General comments:

Questions used to guide interview:

Do you think you are pretty good in _____?

If you had to pick one thing about _____ you liked, what would it be?

If you had to pick one thing about _____ you don't like, what would it be?

What do you do when you are unable to solve a problem or answer a question with your assignment in _____?

Tell me if you think this statement is True or False about you: "I believe I can get better in [skill area] if I work hard and someone teaches me."

Do you enjoy working with other students when you are having trouble with your assignment in _____?

Does the teacher call on you too often? Not often enough? In _____?

From *Academic Skills Problems Fifth Edition Workbook* by Edward S. Shapiro and Nathan H. Clemens. Copyright © 2023 The Guilford Press. Permission to photocopy this form is granted to purchasers of this book for personal use or use with students (see copyright page for details). Purchasers can download additional copies of this form (see the box at the end of the table of contents).

Direct Observation:
Manual for the Behavioral Observation
of Students in Schools (BOSS)

Systematically observing students in classrooms is an important part of the assessment of the instructional environment. This is true whether the referral problem is not completing assignments, having difficulties in reading, or being unable to quickly and accurately compute addition facts.

Although learning to conduct systematic observations is not difficult, it does take some concentrated practice and effort to master the method. It is a rare person (if such a person exists) who can put on a pair of skis for the first time and go schussing down the slopes of Killington in Vermont. It is an equally rare person who can get in front of a group of third-grade children and teach subtraction with regrouping. Attaining the skills to be a good skier or a good teacher takes practice. Learning these skills requires studying persons who are considered experts at the skills in question, trying out the new skills under supervision of such experts, receiving feedback regarding one's performance, and then practicing the newly learned skills.

This manual describes the rationale and process of direct observation. In particular, the use of the BOSS, a measure designed specifically for direct observation of academic skills, is presented.

RATIONALE

Systematic direct observation is defined as a form of quantitative data collection. Its main purpose is the numerical recording of behaviors occurring in the observational setting. For example, if Roberta is reported as not paying attention, systematic observation may show that she was off-task 50% of the time. If Jason is reported as not completing his work, then systematic observation may find that, on average, Jason completes only two of five in-class math assignments per day. If Miguel is reported as fighting on the playground at recess, systematic observation may reveal that he was sent to the principal for fighting five times in the past 2 weeks. In each case, the use of systematic observation is an attempt to capture the quantitative aspects of the behavior taking place.

Of course, teachers and other professionals are constantly observing children in schools; this form of observation provides a subjective impression of a child's behavior. These impressions are important and meaningful, and can be viewed as helpful data in making sense of a child's classroom behavior. Unfortunately, although these subjective impressions are frequently accurate, they can also be inaccurate. For example, Marcus may be reported by a teacher to be a disruptive child due to his frequent teasing of peers. Such a report suggests that the behavior occurs frequently and should be easily observable. If asked to complete a rating scale that includes items about teasing, the teacher may report that the behavior occurs often, when, in reality, the behavior may occur one or two times per class period. However, the fact that the behavior is viewed as negative and obnoxious by the teacher may make it seem like it occurs more frequently. Another teacher may report that Jamie is off-task "all the time." Certainly, although Jamie's off-task behavior may be frequent, it is unlikely that she is off-task all the time. Using a form of systematic observation makes it possible to describe the teasing or off-task occasions objectively, in terms of their frequency. Of course, even a low frequency of misbehavior can be very troubling; teasing that occurs once per week may be viewed as out of line and needing to be stopped. However, knowing that the problem is not as severe as one first thought may be very important in deciding how to best perceive the problem. Systematic observation of Jamie may reveal that she is actually off-task at the same rate as her peers. If that is the case, why does the teacher perceive her to have such a high frequency of inattentiveness? Using systematic observation, one can report, in a quantifiable way, the nature of the off-task behavior that has led the teacher to develop such a perception.

There are several reasons for conducting systematic observations. First, as already noted, getting subjective opinions about behavior is important because these perceptions represent how persons who deal with the problem experience it; indeed, they form the basis of what we think is going on. However, subjective perceptions need to be systematically confirmed or disconfirmed. In addition, as suggested earlier, the problem may be either less or more severe than originally indicated. Thus, two important reasons for conducting systematic observation are the need to confirm or disconfirm subjective reports and to determine the exact severity of the reported problem.

A third reason for conducting systematic observation is to provide a baseline or benchmark against which to assess the success or failure of an instructional intervention. Whenever changes in behavior occur, it is important to document the relative impact of the intervention by comparing the student's present performance with their performance prior to the intervention. This comparison allows the teacher, the student, and the parents to see the gains (or losses) in performance that have occurred over time. It is also required in some states that such baseline data be obtained as part of the evaluation process.

A final reason to collect systematic observation data is to provide feedback to parties (parents, students, teachers, and other school professionals) regarding the types and levels of problems students are currently having. By using systematic observation, interested persons can see how behavior changes in the classroom. Indeed, in the evaluation of students being considered for eligibility as having a specific learning disability, current law requires that observational data be collected that reflect student behavior in their learning environment, including the general education classroom. Systematic direct observation, as described here, would meet this requirement.

IDENTIFYING THE BEHAVIORS FOR OBSERVATION

Systematic observation requires that the behaviors to be observed are carefully and precisely defined. Behaviors that are defined too broadly may be difficult to observe accurately. At the same time, behaviors defined too narrowly may not be meaningful units of responding. The key to effectively identifying behaviors for observation is to think about which ones are likely to be the most relevant to the problem(s) of interest in the classroom.

The literature has suggested that when the problem lies in the area of academics, the observation of *student academic engaged time* is a critical variable. Strong and significant relationships have been identified between high levels of academic engagement and successful academic performance. The relationships suggest a need for a careful analysis of the types of engagement and nonengagement that students exhibit in classrooms (see Chapters 2 and 3 of *Academic Skills Problems, Fifth Edition,* for a more detailed discussion).

The BOSS includes two categories of engagement and three categories of nonengagement. An additional category, which examines the types of instruction occurring in the classroom, is also included in the code. When the interaction of the student's engaged and nonengaged time is examined, a clear picture of the student's behavior in a context of meaningful academic outcomes can be obtained.

GUIDELINES FOR PAPER-AND-PENCIL DIRECT OBSERVATION

Materials

- Two sharp pencils or fine-point pens.
- Clipboard.
- Timing device: Use of an audio- or tactile-cueing device allows the observer to maintain vigilance to the classroom while simultaneously recording with accuracy. Several free "looping" interval timers are available through the app stores for Apple and Google (search for "interval timer" or "looping timer"). The app should offer the capability to signal at 15 seconds repeatedly. Headphones, or the vibrate feature on the device, can be used to hear the audio cue.
- BOSS coding sheet(s) permitting up to 30 minutes of observation. Each minute is divided into four intervals of 15 seconds each. An observation sheet is provided for use with the BOSS, consisting of 180 intervals (60 per page) for a total of 45 minutes (Form 5).

Classroom Etiquette

- Before observing in a classroom, the observer will need to become familiar with the daily schedule, routine, and physical layout of the classroom.
- The observer should meet briefly with the teacher before the observation to learn about classroom rules or procedures that may be in effect during the observation.
- The observer should ask the teacher the best place to sit or stand, so as to be able to observe the target student directly.
- The observer needs to have a clear view of the student, but should not be too obtrusive, and should be sure to stay out of major traffic areas for other students.
- During the observation, the teacher should teach as they normally do.
- The observer should minimize any interactions with students or the teacher during the observation period.
- The teacher should not introduce the observer to the class when they arrive, but should be instructed to tell the students (prior to the observer's arrival) that someone will be coming to observe what goes on in the classroom.
- If the assessment includes working individually with the target student, it is recommended that the direct observation be conducted before the observer meets individually with the student.
- The observer's entrance into the classroom should be as naturalistic as possible. It can help if they enter the classroom during a natural break in the instructional routine.

COMPLETING IDENTIFYING INFORMATION

The coding sheet used with the BOSS (Form 5) is included at the end of this section of the workbook. At the top of the BOSS coding sheet, the observer should be sure to write in the child's name, date, their own name, and the subject matter being observed. In addition, the observer is asked to note the type of instructional setting observed. The time of the observation, along with the length of the observation intervals, should also be recorded.

- *ISW:TPsnt (student in independent seatwork, teacher present):* In this setting, the student is doing independent seatwork while the teacher is available to assist individual children. Typically, the teacher is circulating around the room.
- *ISW:TSmGP (student in independent seatwork, teacher in small group not including target student):* This setting is marked when the target student is engaged in independent seatwork and the teacher is working with a small group that *does not* include the target student.
- *SmGp:Tled (student in small group led by teacher):* This setting is marked when the target student is in a small group (defined as eight or fewer students) that is led by the teacher.

- *LgGp:Tled (student in large group led by teacher):* This setting is marked when the target student is in a large group (defined as more than eight students) that is led by the teacher.
- *Other:* When "Other" is used, the type of instructional setting should be noted in the margin.

The classroom setting is marked by circling the appropriate designation. If the instructional activity changes during the course of the observation, this change should be noted on the observation form by circling the interval where the change occurred and writing in the type of setting that is now in place.

OBSERVING PEER-COMPARISON STUDENTS

A behavioral observation is more meaningful if the target student's behavior is compared to the same behaviors displayed by peers. The BOSS requires that data be collected not only on the target student but also on peers in the same classroom. As noted on the BOSS observation form, every fifth interval is shaded. During each of these intervals, observations are conducted on a randomly selected peer rather than the target student. Before beginning the observation, the observer should decide the sequence of peer-comparison observations. For example, the observer may decide to start in the front left of the classroom and observe a different peer each fifth interval, moving down the row and then from back to front. In truth, it does not matter in which order the peer-comparison data are collected. It does help, however, for the observer to have thought out an observation plan before beginning the observation of the target student.

Data from intervals in which different peers were observed are combined to derive a peer-comparison score for each of the behaviors.

CODING ACADEMIC ENGAGEMENT

The BOSS divides academic engagement into two subcategories: active or passive engaged time. In either case, the student is considered to be on-task. Each of these behaviors is recorded as a momentary time sample. At the beginning of each cued interval, the observer looks at the targeted student; determines whether the student is on-task; and, if so, whether the on-task behavior constitutes an active or passive form of engagement, as defined below. The occurrence of the behavior at that moment is recorded by making a mark in the appropriate box on the scoring sheet.

Active Engaged Time

Active engaged time (AET) is defined as those times when the student is actively attending to the assigned work. Examples of AET include the following:

- Writing
- Reading aloud

- Raising a hand
- Talking to the teacher about the assigned material
- Talking to a peer about the assigned material
- Looking up a word in a dictionary

AET *should not* be scored if the student is:

- Talking about nonacademic material (Verbal Off-Task)
- Walking to the worksheet bin (Motor Off-Task)
- Calling out (Verbal Off-Task), unless it is considered an appropriate response style for that classroom
- Aimlessly flipping the pages of a book (Motor Off-Task)
- Any other form of off-task behavior

Passive Engaged Time

Passive engaged time (PET) is defined as those times when the student is passively attending to assigned work. Examples of PET include the following:

- Listening to a lecture
- Looking at an academic worksheet
- Reading assigned material silently
- Looking at the blackboard during teacher instruction
- Listening to a peer respond to a question

PET *should not* be scored if the student is:

- Aimlessly looking around the classroom (Passive Off-Task)
- Silently reading unassigned material (Passive Off-Task)
- Any other form of off-task behavior

At times it may be difficult to determine immediately whether the child is passively engaged or daydreaming at the first moment of an interval. In this case, it is appropriate to code PET if it becomes apparent later during that interval that the student was indeed passively engaged.

CODING NONENGAGEMENT

When a student is not engaged in academic behavior, three possible categories of off-task behavior are coded. These behaviors are recorded using a partial-interval observation method. If any of the three behaviors occurs at any point during the interval, a mark is made in the appropriate box. Multiple occurrences of the same behavior within a single interval are noted only one time.

Off-Task Motor

Off-Task Motor behaviors (OFT-M) are defined as any instance of motor activity that is not directly associated with an assigned academic task. Examples of OFT-M include the following:

- Engaging in any out-of-seat behavior (defined as a student's buttocks not being in contact with the seat)
- Aimlessly flipping the pages of a book
- Manipulating objects not related to the academic task (e.g., playing with a paper clip, throwing paper, twirling a pencil, folding paper)
- Physically touching another student when not related to an academic task
- Bending or reaching, such as picking up a pencil off the floor
- Drawing or writing that is not related to an assigned academic activity
- Turning around in one's seat, orienting away from the classroom instruction
- Fidgeting in one's seat (i.e., engaging in repetitive motor movements for at least 3 consecutive seconds; student must be off-task for this category to be scored)

OFT-M *should not* be scored if the student is:

- Passing paper to a student, as instructed by the teacher
- Coloring on an assigned worksheet, as instructed (AET)
- Laughing at a joke told by another student (Off-Task Verbal)
- Swinging feet while working on assigned material (AET or PET)

Off-Task Verbal

Off-Task Verbal behaviors (OFT-V) are defined as any audible verbalizations that are not permitted and/or are not related to an assigned academic task. Examples of OFT-V include the following:

- Making any audible sound, such as whistling, humming, or forced burping
- Talking to another student about issues unrelated to an assigned academic task
- Talking to another student about an assigned academic task when such talk is prohibited by the teacher
- Making unauthorized comments or remarks
- Calling out answers to academic problems when the teacher has not specifically asked for an answer or permitted such behavior

OFT-V *should not* be scored if the student is:

- Laughing at a joke told by the teacher
- Talking to another student about the assigned academic work during a cooperative learning group (AET)
- Calling out the answer to a problem when the teacher has permitted such behavior during instruction (AET)

Off-Task Passive

Off-Task Passive behaviors (OFT-P) are defined as those times when a student is passively not attending to an assigned academic activity for a period of at least 3 consecutive seconds. Included are those times when a student is quietly waiting after the completion of an assigned task but is not engaged in an activity authorized by the teacher. Examples of OFT-P behavior include the following:

- Sitting quietly in an unassigned activity
- Looking around the room
- Staring out the window
- Passively listening to other students talk about issues unrelated to the assigned academic activity

It is important to note that the student must be passively off-task for 3-consecutive seconds *within an interval* to be scored. Should the interval end before the full 3-second period occurs, OFT-P is not scored for that interval, and a new consecutive 3-second period is required for the next interval. For instance, suppose a student begins to stare out the window during the third interval of observation. The observer counts only 2 seconds before the fourth interval begins. The student continues to stare out the window for over 3 seconds in this interval. In this case, only the fourth interval would be scored for OFT-P. If the student had stopped staring out the window after 2 seconds of the fourth interval, then OFT-P *should not* have been scored for either interval. In addition, OFT-P *should not* be scored if the student is:

- Quietly reading an assigned book (PET)
- Passively listening to other students talk about the assigned work in a cooperative learning group (PET)

CODING TEACHER-DIRECTED INSTRUCTION

Teacher-directed instruction (TDI) is coded every fifth interval, again by means of a partial-interval observation method. The purpose of these observations is to provide a sampling of time in which the teacher is actively engaged in direct instruction of the classroom. TDI is defined as those times when the teacher is directly instructing the class or individuals within the class. Examples of TDI include times when the teacher is:

- Instructing the whole class or group
- Demonstrating academic material at the board
- Individually assisting a student with an assigned task

TDI should not be scored if the teacher is:

- Scolding the class or an individual student for misbehavior
- Giving instructions for an academic activity

- Sitting at their desk grading papers
- Speaking to an individual student or the class about nonacademic issues

REVIEW:
PROCEDURE FOR CONDUCTING THE OBSERVATION

After the observer is seated in the classroom, they begin the observation by starting the interval timer. At the signal for the first interval (and each interval signal thereafter), the observer immediately records whether the student is actively or passively engaged in academic behavior. If the student is off-task at the moment that the cue occurred, the observer leaves the boxes blank or does not score either AET or PET. For the remainder of the interval, the observer watches to see if the student engages in any form of off-task behavior. Before the next interval begins, if the student gets out of their seat and then talks to another student about nonacademic issues, marks would be made in the OFT-M and OFT-V columns of interval 1. The process is repeated until the observer reaches interval 5. Having decided to start with the students in the first row of desks for purposes of peer-comparison data collection, upon hearing the signal for interval 5, the observer now looks to see whether the student sitting in the first row, left side of the room, is on-task. That student is now observed for any off-task behavior throughout the remainder of the interval. In addition, during the fifth interval, the observer records whether the teacher engaged in any direct instruction. When the sixth interval begins, the observer returns to watching and recording the behavior of the target student. This process is repeated until the observation is completed. Figure 3 displays a completed sample observation using the BOSS.

SCORING THE BOSS

All categories of the BOSS are scored using the same metric: percentage of intervals in which the behavior occurred. Hand scoring requires that the number of intervals in which the behavior was marked as occurring be divided by the total number of intervals of observing the student, and multiplying the result by 100.

- **Step 1.** Add the number of times each behavior occurred for the target student *only*, across the rows. Enter this number on the data collection sheet in the corresponding cell under the column marked "S" (for target student). Be sure *not* to add the number of occurrences in the intervals during which peer-comparison data were collected (see Figure 4).
    As can be seen in Figure 4, the target student was observed to have engaged in AET for 5 out of the first 15 intervals observed, PET for 5, OFT-M for 2, OFT-V for 3, and OFT-P for 3.

- **Step 2.** Add up the number of intervals each behavior is observed for the target student across the entire observation, and record the total in the lower left portion of the form. This is done by simply adding the "S" row totals for each behavior.

Behavioral Observation of Students in Schools (BOSS)

Child Observed: __Justin__ Academic Subject: __Math__

Date: __9/15/20__ Setting: ____ ISW:TPsnt __X__ SmGp:TPsnt

Observer: __JGL__ ____ ISW:TSmGp ____ LgGp:TPsnt

Time of Observation: __10:30__ Interval Length: __15__ Other: _____

Moment	1	2	3	4	5*	6	7	8	9	10*	11	12	13	14	15*	S	P	T
AET	\		\		\	\	\			\						5	2	
PET		\						\	\		\			\	\	5	1	
Partial																		
OFT-M	\								\						\	2	1	
OFT-V						\	\			\	\					3	1	
OFT-P	\			\	\											3	1	
TDI															\			1

Moment	16	17	18	19	20*	21	22	23	24	25*	26	27	28	29	30*	S	P	T
AET	\			\							\				\	3	1	
PET			\		\	\						\				3	1	
Partial																		
OFT-M		\														1	0	
OFT-V		\								\						1	1	
OFT-P							\	\	\					\	\	5	0	
TDI					\					\					\			3

Moment	31	32	33	34	35*	36	37	38	39	40*	41	42	43	44	45*	S	P	T
AET		\			\											1	1	
PET	\		\	\							\	\	\	\		7	0	
Partial																		
OFT-M								\	\						\	2	1	
OFT-V						\	\									2	0	
OFT-P										\						0	1	
TDI										\					\			2

Moment	46	47	48	49	50*	51	52	53	54	55*	56	57	58	59	60*	S	P	T
AET					\											0	1	
PET		\	\	\						\					\	3	2	
Partial																		
OFT-M											\					1	0	
OFT-V											\	\				2	0	
OFT-P						\	\	\	\					\		5	0	
TDI															\			1

	Target Student			*Peer Comparison			Teacher	
	S AET	9	% AET 18.8	S AET	5	% AET 41.7	S TDI	7
Total	S PET	18	% PET 37.5	S PET	4	% PET 33.3	% TDI	58.3
Intervals	S OFT-M	6	% OFT-M 12.5	S OFT-M	2	% OFT-M 16.7	Total Intervals	
Observed	S OFT-V	8	% OFT-V 16.7	S OFT-V	2	% OFT-V 16.7	Observed	12
48	OFT-P	13	% OFT-P 27.1	S OFT-P	2	% OFT-P 16.7		

FIGURE 3. Completed BOSS observation on Justin.

30

Moment	1	2	3	4	5*	6	7	8	9	10*	11	12	13	14	15*	S	P	T
AET	\		\		\	\	\			\		\				5	1	
PET		\						\	\		\			\	\	5	2	
Partial																		
OFT-M	\								\						\	2	0	
OFT-V						\	\			\	\					3	0	
OFT-P	\			\	\								\			3	0	
TDI					\										\			1

FIGURE 4. First 15 intervals of BOSS observation for Justin. *, peer comparison.

• **Step 3.** Determine the total number of intervals in which the target student was observed and record this number in the space provided in the lower left portion of the data collection sheet. Again, be sure to eliminate any intervals in which the peer-comparison data were collected.

As evident in Figure 3, the target student was observed for a total of 48 intervals during this observation.

• **Step 4.** Divide the number of occurrences of each behavior by the total intervals observed and multiply by 100. This is the percentage of intervals in which the behavior was observed to occur. Record this percentage in the spaces provided.

• **Step 5.** Repeat this process, but now calculate only the intervals in which peer-comparison data (P) were collected. Eliminate any intervals in which the target student was observed (see Figure 5).

• **Step 6.** Repeat the process one more time, but now examine only the intervals in which TDI data were collected (see Figure 6). Eliminate any intervals in which the target student data were collected. Note that the intervals in which peer-comparison data were collected are the same ones in which TDI is observed.

In the example shown in Figure 3, the target student was observed for a total of 48 intervals, peers for 12 intervals. Across the observation, AET for the target student was observed nine times, resulting in 18.8% of the intervals. For the

Moment	1	2	3	4	5*	6	7	8	9	10*	11	12	13	14	15*	S	P	T
AET	\		\		\	\	\			\		\				5	2	
PET		\						\	\		\			\	\	5	1	
Partial																		
OFT-M	\								\						\	2	1	
OFT-V						\	\			\	\					3	1	
OFT-P	\			\	\								\			3	1	
TDI					\										\			1

FIGURE 5. First 15 intervals of BOSS observation for Justin, scored for peer-comparison students. *, peer comparison.

Moment	1	2	3	4	5*	6	7	8	9	10*	11	12	13	14	15*	S	P	T
AET	\		\		\	\	\			\		\				5	2	
PET		\						\	\		\			\	\	5	1	
Partial																		
OFT-M	\								\						\	2	1	
OFT-V						\	\			\	\					3	1	
OFT-P	\			\	\								\			3	1	
TDI					\										\			2

FIGURE 6. First 15 intervals of BOSS observation for Justin, scored for TDI. *, peer comparison.

peer-comparison students, AET was observed five times out of 12 intervals, or 41.7% of the intervals. Calculations for all categories should result in the summary on the bottom of Figure 3.

INTERPRETATION OF BOSS DATA

Interpretation of the BOSS data can involve analysis of several aspects of classroom behavior. First, the BOSS shows the levels of academic engagement and nonengagement for the targeted student in the particular setting of observation. By comparing the combined percentages of AET and PET against those of the three OFT categories, the observer can establish the amount of a student's on- and off-task behavior. These data can provide the observer with information about the extent to which the target student is effectively engaged in the learning process.

Second, observations across multiple settings make it possible to determine relative differences in the target student's academic engagement in different instructional environments. For example, it may be found that a student has much higher levels of on-task behavior when they are in a teacher-led setting than when involved in independent seatwork.

Third, by examining the relative differences between AET and PET, the observer can determine whether the opportunities to respond (AET level) for a student are of a sufficient number to provide clear evidence of academic progress. Students who are struggling in school are often found to have relatively low levels of AET even when they are on-task.

Fourth, and most importantly, the observer can compare the performance of the target student against the student's peers. Use of this type of local normative data is crucial in understanding the degree to which the levels of behavior obtained for the target student differ from the expected performance of the student's classmates. At times, a student who appears to have very low levels of on-task behavior may be found to have a level equivalent to those of their peers, suggesting that the student's behavior may not be beyond the expectations set by the classroom teacher. On the other hand, a student appearing to have very high levels of on-task behavioral performance may be viewed as not meeting classroom expectations. When comparisons are made to the student's peers, it may become evident that although the student's level is high, it is significantly lower than the levels of their peers.

One of the most frequently asked questions related to conducting systematic observation is, "How much observation is needed?" The answer is, "It depends." Accurate observations require at least 10–15 minutes. Optimally, observations should be 20–30 minutes each. In the best of all possible worlds, the observation should be repeated over 2–3 days and possibly across different types of academic settings (e.g., independent work in reading, small-group activities in math, large-group activities in science). Obviously, the practical restrictions of time may limit how much observation can be done. So, the question is whether a single observation can be enough.

The key to good observation is that it accurately represents the child's behavior at the time of the observation and at other times of the day. If a child's behavior tends to be highly variable from day to day or hour to hour, a single observation at one time in one setting may not be sufficient. Likewise, if a child's behavior changes because there is an observer in the classroom, or the child is having a "good day," a single observation may not be enough. Certainly, some degree of stable responding from day to day is important; however, the problem of some children is precisely that they are inconsistent, so expecting consistency in those cases is unrealistic.

One way to address this problem is always to ask the teacher whether the behavior seen that day was typical of the student's performance. If it was, then the one observation may be enough. However, if the child's behavior was atypical of what the teacher thinks is their usual behavior, then additional observation is needed.

Another important issue to consider in deciding whether enough observation has been done is whether the situation in which the behavior was observed represents where the problems tend to occur. For example, although the teacher notes that Justin has problems during independent seatwork activities, an important question for the teacher is whether there are equal problems in math and reading. One hypothesis about Justin's behavior may be that his skill levels differ across subject matter, and the differential skill levels result in differential behavioral outcomes. Thus, it may be crucial to conduct observations during independent seatwork periods in both math and reading activities.

In the example shown in Figure 3, the student Justin was observed during his math class. Throughout the observation, the teacher was engaged in teaching a small group (six students) in which Justin was included. Peer-comparison data for this observation were collected among the other five students in Justin's small group. The observation lasted for 15 minutes and was conducted at 10:30 A.M. Justin's overall level of on-task behavior is much lower than that of his peers. In total, Justin was academically engaged for 56.3% of the observed intervals, whereas his peers remained engaged for 75.0% of the observed intervals. In addition, when Justin was engaged, he spent the largest proportion of his time (37.5% of the intervals) in passive rather than active forms of engagement. In contrast, his peers were actively engaged for 41.7% of the intervals.

When Justin was off-task, he was primarily nonengaged in passive ways. Typically, this involved looking away from his work and staring out the windows, but also included his getting out of his seat and speaking to his peers. However, these off-task behaviors by Justin were comparable to those of his classmates.

Justin's teacher was engaged in directed teaching activities for approximately 58.3% of the observed intervals. During intervals when Justin's teacher was not instructing the class, she was observed in classroom management activities, such as redirecting Justin and other students to pay attention to her direction.

Regarding interpreting data from the BOSS, it is important to note that the observer does not view the level of behavior obtained through the observation to represent an estimate of the amount of time that a behavior would occur. Because the observation system is derived from a time-sampling strategy, it would be inaccurate to say that the behavior occurred for X% of the time. This is especially true since partial-interval recording systems (such as those used here for the off-task behaviors and TDI) are likely to overestimate the actual rate of a behavior's occurrence. It is also important to note that the data collected for the target student are likely to be more reliable and stable then the data collected for peer-comparison purposes. The more observation intervals, the better the stability of the measure. In this observation example, there were 48 observations of the target student and only 12 of the peers. Data collected on peers must be considered cautiously in the interpretation of results.

Behavioral Observation of Students in Schools (BOSS)

Child Observed: _____   Academic Subject: _____

Date: _____   Setting: _____ ISW:TPsnt _____ SmGp:TPsnt

Observer: _____   _____ ISW:TSmGp _____ LgGp:TPsnt

Time of Observation: _____   Interval Length: _____ Other: _____

Moment	1	2	3	4	5*	6	7	8	9	10*	11	12	13	14	15*	S	P	T
AET																		
PET																		
Partial																		
OFT-M																		
OFT-V																		
OFT-P																		
TDI																		

Moment	16	17	18	19	20*	21	22	23	24	25*	26	27	28	29	30*	S	P	T
AET																		
PET																		
Partial																		
OFT-M																		
OFT-V																		
OFT-P																		
TDI																		

Moment	31	32	33	34	35*	36	37	38	39	40*	41	42	43	44	45*	S	P	T
AET																		
PET																		
Partial																		
OFT-M																		
OFT-V																		
OFT-P																		
TDI																		

Moment	46	47	48	49	50*	51	52	53	54	55*	56	57	58	59	60*	S	P	T
AET																		
PET																		
Partial																		
OFT-M																		
OFT-V																		
OFT-P																		
TDI																		

	Target Student			*Peer Comparison			Teacher	
Total Intervals Observed	S AET _____	% AET _____	S AET _____	% AET _____	S TDI _____	% TDI _____	
	S PET _____	% PET _____	S PET _____	% PET _____			
	S OFT-M _____	% OFT-M _____	S OFT-M _____	% OFT-M _____	Total Intervals Observed _____		
	S OFT-V _____	% OFT-V _____	S OFT-V _____	% OFT-V _____			
_____	OFT-P _____	% OFT-P _____	S OFT-P _____	% OFT-P _____			

(continued)

From *Academic Skills Problems Fifth Edition Workbook* by Edward S. Shapiro and Nathan H. Clemens. Copyright © 2023 The Guilford Press. Permission to photocopy this form is granted to purchasers of this book for personal use or use with students (see copyright page for details). Purchasers can download additional copies of this form (see the box at the end of the table of contents).

Behavioral Observation of Students in Schools (BOSS)

Child Observed: _____   Academic Subject: _____

Date: _____   Setting: _____ ISW:TPsnt _____ SmGp:TPsnt

Observer: _____   _____ ISW:TSmGp _____ LgGp:TPsnt

Time of Observation: _____   Interval Length: _____ Other: _____

Moment	61	62	63	64	65*	66	67	68	69	70*	71	72	73	74	75*	S	P	T
AET																		
PET																		
Partial																		
OFT-M																		
OFT-V																		
OFT-P																		
TDI																		

Moment	76	77	78	79	80*	81	82	83	84	85*	86	87	88	99	90*	S	P	T
AET																		
PET																		
Partial																		
OFT-M																		
OFT-V																		
OFT-P																		
TDI																		

Moment	91	92	93	94	95*	96	97	98	99	100*	101	102	103	104	105*	S	P	T
AET																		
PET																		
Partial																		
OFT-M																		
OFT-V																		
OFT-P																		
TDI																		

Moment	106	107	108	109	110*	111	112	113	114	115*	116	117	118	119	120*	S	P	T
AET																		
PET																		
Partial																		
OFT-M																		
OFT-V																		
OFT-P																		
TDI																		

	Target Student			*Peer Comparison			Teacher	
Total	S AET _____	% AET _____		S AET _____	% AET _____		S TDI	_____
Intervals	S PET _____	% PET _____		S PET _____	% PET _____		% TDI	_____
Observed	S OFT-M _____	% OFT-M _____		S OFT-M _____	% OFT-M _____		Total Intervals	
	S OFT-V _____	% OFT-V _____		S OFT-V _____	% OFT-V _____		Observed	_____
_____	OFT-P _____	% OFT-P _____		S OFT-P _____	% OFT-P _____			

(continued)

Behavioral Observation of Students in Schools (BOSS)

Child Observed: _____   Academic Subject: _____

Date: _____   Setting: _____ ISW:TPsnt _____ SmGp:TPsnt

Observer: _____   _____ ISW:TSmGp _____ LgGp:TPsnt

Time of Observation: _____   Interval Length: _____ Other: _____

Moment	121	122	123	124	125*	126	127	128	129	130*	131	132	133	134	135*	S	P	T
AET																		
PET																		
Partial																		
OFT-M																		
OFT-V																		
OFT-P																		
TDI																		

Moment	136	137	138	139	140*	141	142	143	144	145*	146	147	148	149	150*	S	P	T
AET																		
PET																		
Partial																		
OFT-M																		
OFT-V																		
OFT-P																		
TDI																		

Moment	151	152	153	154	155*	156	157	158	159	160*	161	162	163	164	165*	S	P	T
AET																		
PET																		
Partial																		
OFT-M																		
OFT-V																		
OFT-P																		
TDI																		

Moment	166	167	168	169	170*	171	172	173	174	175*	176	177	178	179	180*	S	P	T
AET																		
PET																		
Partial																		
OFT-M																		
OFT-V																		
OFT-P																		
TDI																		

	Target Student		*Peer Comparison		Teacher	
Total	S AET _____	% AET _____	S AET _____	% AET _____	S TDI _____	
Intervals	S PET _____	% PET _____	S PET _____	% PET _____	% TDI _____	
Observed	S OFT-M _____	% OFT-M _____	S OFT-M _____	% OFT-M _____	Total Intervals	
	S OFT-V _____	% OFT-V _____	S OFT-V _____	% OFT-V _____	Observed _____	
_____	OFT-P _____	% OFT-P _____	S OFT-P _____	% OFT-P _____		

Direct Observation:
Behavioral Observation of Students
in Schools—Modified (BOSS-M)

The BOSS is a valuable tool for school-based practice. However, after conducting hundreds of direct observations with the BOSS and similar variations, training students and research staff to use it, and talking with school psychologists, there is room for an alternative that captures behaviors critical for academic functioning but in a simplified way. The BOSS—Modified (BOSS-M) is an adapted, alternate version of the BOSS code and can be found in Form 6 at the end of this section.

There are two main behaviors recorded on the BOSS-M:

- **On-Task.** This collapses behaviors coded as AET and PET on the standard BOSS into one behavior. It is defined as: *Student behavior that meets expectations for the situation (e.g., engaged with assigned task, attending to teacher or relevant work, waiting appropriately)*. Like AET and PET, it is coded using momentary time sampling at the start of each interval. The reason for coding "on-task" as a single variable as opposed to coding active and passive forms of engagement is as follows. First, there are occasions in which differences in AET and PET across settings may be difficult to interpret, or have low utility in reflecting the student's engagement or opportunities for active engagement in the academic environment. Low rates of AET demonstrated by the student do not necessarily mean there were few opportunities for active engagement. Second, differences in AET and PET demonstrated by the student may not matter as much as the *overall* level of engagement. Although active engagement is certainly important for learning and maintaining students' attention, passive engagement is still valuable and may be the only option in some situations. Therefore, there are times when simply coding engagement, regardless if it is active or passive, is sufficient for answering questions regarding the on-task behavior for a student across instructional situations.

39

• **Disruptive.** Rather than code different types of off-task behaviors as on the standard BOSS, disruptive behavior is coded on the BOSS-M. It is defined as: *Student action that interrupts classroom activity, interferes with instruction, or distracts other students (e.g., out of seat, playing with objects that distract others, acting aggressively, talking/yelling about things that are unrelated to classroom instruction).* Like the off-task behaviors on the standard BOSS, disruptive is coded using partial-interval recording at any point in the interval. The rationale for coding disruptive behavior is that, on the standard BOSS, the resulting data on the off-task behaviors sometimes simply reflect the inverse of engagement. In contrast to a lack of engagement (which is already captured in the BOSS-M by On-Task), disruptive behaviors interfere with learning, both for the target student, as well as potentially the teacher's instruction. Coding disruptive behaviors thereby makes the observation data more comprehensive by capturing behaviors that are more impactful to the learning environment than just off-task behavior, and helps capture the nature and severity of the target student's difficulties (and their effects on the instructional setting).

Much of the observation structure on the BOSS-M is the same as the standard BOSS. It uses the same 15-second interval structure and maintains options for collecting peer-comparison data every fifth interval.

Studies of the BOSS-M are currently ongoing, so users are cautioned to view this as a pilot version.

Behavior Observation of Students in Schools—Modified

Student _____ Date _____ School _____

Teacher _____ Time Start _____ Time End _____

Subject Observed and Activity _____ Grouping/Format _____

On-Task: Momentary time sample (score at start of interval). ***Student behavior that meets expectations for the situation (e.g., engaged with assigned task, attending to teacher or relevant work, waiting appropriately).***

Disruptive: Partial interval (score any time during interval). ***Student action that interrupts classroom activity, interferes with instruction, or distracts other students (e.g., out of seat, playing with objects that distract others, acting aggressively, talking/yelling about things that are unrelated to classroom instruction).***

Every fifth interval: Observe comparison peer (optional)

15-second intervals

	1	2	3	4	5	6	7	8	9	10	11	12	13	14	15	16	17	18	19	20
On-Task																				
Disruptive																				

	21	22	23	24	25	26	27	28	29	30	31	32	33	34	35	36	37	38	39	40
On-Task																				
Disruptive																				

	41	42	43	44	45	46	47	48	49	50	51	52	53	54	55	56	57	58	59	60
On-Task																				
Disruptive																				

	61	62	63	64	65	66	67	68	69	70	71	72	73	74	75	76	77	78	79	80
On-Task																				
Disruptive																				

	81	82	83	84	85	86	87	88	89	90	91	92	93	94	95	96	97	98	99	100
On-Task																				
Disruptive																				

		# Intervals Occurred	# Intervals Observed	Percentage (occurred / observed) × 100
Target Student	On-Task			
	Disruptive			
Peer Comparisons	On-Task			
	Disruptive			

Comments _____

_____

From *Academic Skills Problems Fifth Edition Workbook* by Edward S. Shapiro and Nathan H. Clemens. Copyright © 2023 The Guilford Press. Permission to photocopy this form is granted to purchasers of this book for personal use or use with students (see copyright page for details). Purchasers can download additional copies of this form (see the box at the end of the table of contents).

Assessing Instructional Placement

Reading

In a direct assessment of reading, oral reading (i.e., oral reading fluency) is commonly used as an index of reading achievement and for assessing student progress. However, this metric is only one of several that can be used for conducting a curriculum-based assessment of reading, and some may be used as adjuncts, or in place of oral reading.

A maze measure for assessing reading is available from several vendors (see the academic progress monitoring tools charts maintained by the National Center on Intensive Intervention). Grade-level passages are typically available for grades 1–8. A significant advantage of maze measures is that students take them independently, meaning that multiple students can take them at once. This may be valuable in situations where limited teachers or staff are available for monitoring students' progress, or if staff wishes to minimize disruptions to instruction. Most maze measures are constructed in a similar way: Beginning with the second sentence, every seventh word is removed, with three choices available for the student. One of the words is correct, another is a closely related but incorrect response, and a third is a distractor. Students are asked to circle the correct word as they read the passage. They are given 3 minutes to read the passage, and the number of correct maze words per minute represents the score on the item. Figure 7 provides an example of a paper-and-pencil version of the maze technique. Maze measures are available from several vendors, including DIBELS (*dibels.uoregon.edu*) and Acadience (*acadiencelearning. org*). Normative data are also available from these vendors to interpret the outcomes of student performance on the maze task.

Oral retell techniques may be used as an adjunct to a curriculum-based assessment of reading. In this technique, students are asked to read a passage and then retell what they read in their own words. The task can be done using silent and oral reading if the evaluator suspects that a student is having difficulties when asked to read aloud. The student's responses can be scored using a checklist or rating scale, such as that provided in Form 7 or 8.

On Saturday, our town had a kite flying day. People were invited to bring their (**trees, kites, forks**) to the park. The park had (**a, it, in**) big, open field that was perfect (**see, to, for**) flying kites. It was a beautiful (**day, house, year**). The sun was shining, and there (**it, was, were**) a nice breeze to help the (**dogs, planes, kites**) fly.

Lots of people came to (**fly, bury, throw**) their kites. They brought all sorts (**in, of, to**) kites in all different shapes and (**speeds, feelings, colors**). Some kites were small and other (**kites, birds, cars**) were big. Some kites were shaped (**and, to, like**) a diamond, others were shaped like (**wood, boxes, water**), circles, and even stars. One kite (**be, to, was**) an airplane shape, and another was (**shaped, under, broken**) like a giant bird.

My Dad (**went, found, took**) me to kite day. Our kite (**was, when, it**) blue and had a picture of (**and, is, a**) unicorn. Our kite had long tails (**it, of, to**) different colors, like a rainbow. There (**were, when, they**) lots of people there with their (**cars, brooms, kites**). We found an open spot to (**eat, fly, forget**) our kite. I held the handle. (**My, Me, The**) Dad said to hold on tight (**to, if, so**) that the kite would not fly (**away, inside, for**). He held the kite up high (**if, said, for**) the wind to catch it. The (**cat, kite, balloon**) started to fly. I held on (**tight, when, empty**) to the handle. My Dad told (**Dad, dog, me**) to let out more string to (**cut, make, again**) the kite fly higher. I let (**out, in, fly**) more string and the kite went (**up, under, be**). It went higher and higher. It (**and, was, for**) as high as a bird. It (**was, in, sing**) cool to see all of the (**planes, kites, pigs**) flying in the sky.

FIGURE 7. Example of maze task for grade 2.

Form 7 is used for narrative passages and provides an opportunity to examine whether students know the key elements of story grammar, such as story sense, setting, characters, key events, and resolution. This form can be used for almost any narrative passage.

Form 8 provides a similar scoring rubric for expository or informational passages. The broad categories for scoring this type of retell include examination of the main topic, primary supporting detail, and secondary supporting detail. Users of this form must examine passages that are used for retells and, prior to using the form, establish the primary and secondary supporting details for that specific passage.

ORAL RETELL TECHNIQUES

• **Step 1.** The examiner selects a passage for the student to read. The passage should be between 250 and 300 words for a student in grade 3 or above, or between 150 and 200 words for a student in grade 1 or 2. The passage used should also have a story or theme embedded in it.

• **Step 2.** The examiner asks the student to read the entire passage aloud and times the reading (first minute only) to determine the rate of words read correctly and incorrectly per minute.

• **Step 3.** The examiner then asks the student to retell the passage in their own words and records the response for later scoring. The retell should be done in the following sequence: If the student is able to complete the retell accurately, according to Level A procedures, then Levels B, C, and D would not be done. The examiner should proceed to the next level of the retell technique if the student is unsuccessful at the preceding level.

○ Level A: *Nonprompted retell without passage.* The examiner asks the student to retell the story in the passage, without allowing them access to the passage. When the student cannot add anything else to their retell, they are stopped.

○ Level B: *Nonprompted retell with passage.* The examiner asks the student to retell the story in the passage, allowing them access to the passage. Again, when the student cannot add anything to their retell, they are stopped.

○ Level C: *Prompted retell without passage.* The examiner does not allow the student access to the passage but provides them with a simple prompt about the passage. For example, in the first case example using a narrative passage, the evaluator might ask the student, "The main idea of this story was about a circus coming to town. Now tell me more about the story." The examiner can continue to prompt the student to see how many prompts are needed for the student to accurately recall the information read. The student is stopped when they cannot recall anything further. Similarly, in the second example where the student read an expository passage about flamingos, the evaluator might ask the student, "The main idea of this passage was interesting facts about flamingos. Tell me some things about flamingos you remember that make them special birds." The examiner can continue to prompt the student to see how many prompts are needed for them to provide supporting details to the main idea of the story.

○ Level D: *Prompted retell with access to passage.* The student is allowed to look at the passage as the examiner provides a simple prompt about the story. For example, for the narrative story, the evaluator might say to the student, "The main idea of this story was about a circus coming to town. Now tell me more about the story." Similarly, for the expository story, the examiner might say, "The main idea of this passage was facts about flamingos. Tell me some of the interesting things about flamingos that you read in the passage." Again, the examiner can continue to prompt the student to see how many prompts are needed for them to accurately recall the information read. The student is stopped when they cannot recall anything further.

• **Step 4.** The examiner scores the retell against the retelling scoring form provided or developed for the passage. Again, an example of such a scoring form is provided in Forms 7 and 8.

Another variation of the retell technique would ask the student to read the story silently to themselves rather than aloud.

FORM 7

Quantification of Retelling for Narrative Text

Student's Name: _____

Book/Page: _____ Date: _____

Directions: Place a 1 next to each item the student includes in their retelling. Credit the gist, as well as the obvious recall. Place an * if you ask the child questions to aid recall.

		Level				
		A	B	C	D	
Story sense						
Theme:	Main idea or moral of story	☐	☐	☐	☐	(1)
Problem:	Difficulty to overcome	☐	☐	☐	☐	(1)
Goal:	What the character wants to happen	☐	☐	☐	☐	(1)
Title:	Name of the story (if possible)	☐	☐	☐	☐	(1)
Setting						
	When and where the story occurs	☐	☐	☐	☐	(1)
Characters						
	Name the main characters	☐	☐	☐	☐	(1)
Events/episodes						
	Initiating event	☐	☐	☐	☐	(1)
	Major events (climax)	☐	☐	☐	☐	(1)
	Sequence: retells in structural order	☐	☐	☐	☐	(1)
Resolution						
	Name problem solution for the goal	☐	☐	☐	☐	(.5)
	End of the story	☐	☐	☐	☐	(.5)

TOTAL ____ ____ ____ ____

From *Academic Skills Problems Fifth Edition Workbook* by Edward S. Shapiro and Nathan H. Clemens. Copyright © 2023 The Guilford Press. Permission to photocopy this form is granted to purchasers of this book for personal use or use with students (see copyright page for details). Purchasers can download additional copies of this form (see the box at the end of the table of contents).

Quantification of Retelling for Expository Text

Student's Name: _____

Title of Passage: _____ Date: _____

Instructions:

- Listen to the child's retell up to two times, while referring to the template provided.
- Circle **1** if the child included the item in their retell, and circle **0** if they omitted the item.
- For the "Topic" and "Main Idea" categories, circle **0** if they omitted the item or part of the item listed on the template, and circle **1** if they completely stated the item listed on the template.
- For "Primary Supporting Details" and "Secondary Supporting Details," circle **0** if they omitted the item, **1** if they provided **1** response, **2** if they provided **2** responses, **3** if they provided **3** responses, and **4** if they provided **4 or more** responses.
- Write the "Total Score" on the line provided (**0–10 points**).

Topic: • _____	0 1
Main idea: • _____	0 1
Primary supporting details: • _____ • _____ • _____ • _____ • _____ • _____ • _____ • _____	0 1 2 3 4
Secondary supporting details: • _____ • _____ • _____ • _____ • _____ • _____ • _____ • _____ • _____	0 1 2 3 4

TOTAL SCORE: _____

From *Academic Skills Problems Fifth Edition Workbook* by Edward S. Shapiro and Nathan H. Clemens. Copyright © 2023 The Guilford Press. Permission to photocopy this form is granted to purchasers of this book for personal use or use with students (see copyright page for details). Purchasers can download additional copies of this form (see the box at the end of the table of contents).

RETELL TECHNIQUES: EXAMPLES AND EXERCISES

Case Descriptions: Narrative Retell

Shawn was a fourth-grade student in a general education classroom. He was selected by his teacher as an average-performing student in the classroom. Troy was a fourth-grade student in the same general education classroom as Shawn. His teacher selected him as a student having significant problems in reading. Both students were asked to read the following passage and then to retell the story in their own words, without use of the passage (Level A retell). After reading each student's retell, readers are invited to complete the Quantification of Retelling for Narrative Text form provided for each one (see Exercise 1 and Exercise 2). A completed form is provided on the following page in each case.

Passage Read

The people of Lone Tree, Texas, often wonder why the circus never comes to their town. Almost nobody remembers the one time, years ago, that the circus did come to town.

Lone Tree was a busy cowtown. Two trains stopped there each day. On Saturday night folks from miles around came to town—ranchers, cowboys, Indians, and homesteaders. Bearpaw Smith's store had just about everything that the people needed. But there was one thing missing. None of these people had ever seen the circus.

Then one day a silent stranger came to Lone Tree and plastered the walls of Bearpaw Smith's store with circus posters. The circus was coming to town! The people were so excited, they could hardly wait for the day of the show. The big day finally arrived, and it would be a day to remember.

An hour before showtime the crowd on the midway and around the ticket wagon was already so great that it seemed impossible that the circus tent would be able to hold them all. And still the people came.

One of the latecomers was Clyde Jones, the mountain-lion hunter, with his pack of "lion hounds." The circus people said it was against the rules to take dogs into the tent. Clyde said his were the best hounds in the state and where he went they went. The ticket taker answered that this was one place they were not going to go. If Clyde wanted to see the circus, he'd have to leave his dogs outside. Clyde grumbled, but he did want to see the circus, so he tied the hounds to tent stakes and left them howling after him as he went inside.

Results of Retelling for Shawn

Rates: Words correct/minute = 131
 Words incorrect/minute = 0

Verbatim transcript: "It's about a town in Texas, and they've never seen, like, a circus before, and they want to see it. And they know a store that has everything except for a circus. And one day the store gets plastered, and they find out there is going to be a circus coming, and when they see it they can't believe that everyone can all fit into the tent. And then there is a man that comes late and he has, like, hounds and he can't bring them in, so he just leaves them out. But he wanted to bring them in, but he had to leave them outside."

Instructions: On Exercise 1 (p. 52), score Shawn's retelling for Level A before looking at the scored form on page 53.

Quantification of Retelling for Narrative Text

Student's Name: _____

Book/Page: _____ Date: _____

Directions: Place a 1 next to each item the student includes in their retelling. Credit the gist, as well as the obvious recall. Place an * if you ask the child questions to aid recall.

			Level				
			A	B	C	D	
Story sense							
Theme:	Main idea or moral of story		☐	☐	☐	☐	(1)
Problem:	Difficulty to overcome		☐	☐	☐	☐	(1)
Goal:	What the character wants to happen		☐	☐	☐	☐	(1)
Title:	Name of the story (if possible)		☐	☐	☐	☐	(1)
Setting							
When and where the story occurs			☐	☐	☐	☐	(1)
Characters							
Name the main characters			☐	☐	☐	☐	(1)
Events/episodes							
Initiating event			☐	☐	☐	☐	(1)
Major events (climax)			☐	☐	☐	☐	(1)
Sequence: retells in structural order			☐	☐	☐	☐	(1)
Resolution							
Name problem solution for the goal			☐	☐	☐	☐	(.5)
End of the story			☐	☐	☐	☐	(.5)

TOTAL ____ ____ ____ ____

Quantification of Retelling for Narrative Text

Student's Name: _Shawn_

Book/Page: _____ Date: _____

Directions: Place a 1 next to each item the student includes in their retelling. Credit the gist, as well as the obvious recall. Place an * if you ask the child questions to aid recall.

		Level				
		A	B	C	D	
Story sense						
Theme:	Main idea or moral of story	☒	☐	☐	☐	(1)
Problem:	Difficulty to overcome	☒	☐	☐	☐	(1)
Goal:	What the character wants to happen	☒	☐	☐	☐	(1)
Title:	Name of the story (if possible)	☐	☐	☐	☐	(1)
Setting						
When and where the story occurs		☒	☐	☐	☐	(1)
Characters						
Name the main characters		☐	☐	☐	☐	(1)
Events/episodes						
Initiating event		☒	☐	☐	☐	(1)
Major events (climax)		☒	☐	☐	☐	(1)
Sequence: retells in structural order		☒	☐	☐	☐	(1)
Resolution						
Name problem solution for the goal		☒	☐	☐	☐	(.5)
End the story		☒	☐	☐	☐	(.5)

TOTAL _8_ ___ ___ ___

Comment: Note that Shawn's performance at Level A suggests no need to move to other levels of the retell technique.

Results of Retelling for Troy

Rates: Words correct/minute = 55
Errors/minute = 3

Verbatim transcript: (*Long pause*) "The people are saying there has never been a circus in town before. So one day they heard there was a circus coming to town. Everybody was so happy they couldn't wait for the day to come. (*Examiner: Anything else?*) No."

Instructions: On Exercise 2 (p. 55), score Troy's retelling for Level A before looking at the scored form on page 56.

Quantification of Retelling for Narrative Text

Student's Name: _____

Book/Page: _____ Date: _____

Directions: Place a 1 next to each item the student includes in their retelling. Credit the gist, as well as the obvious recall. Place an * if you ask the child questions to aid recall.

			Level				
			A	B	C	D	
Story sense							
	Theme:	Main idea or moral of story	☐	☐	☐	☐	(1)
	Problem:	Difficulty to overcome	☐	☐	☐	☐	(1)
	Goal:	What the character wants to happen	☐	☐	☐	☐	(1)
	Title:	Name of the story (if possible)	☐	☐	☐	☐	(1)
Setting							
	When and where the story occurs		☐	☐	☐	☐	(1)
Characters							
	Name the main characters		☐	☐	☐	☐	(1)
Events/episodes							
	Initiating event		☐	☐	☐	☐	(1)
	Major events (climax)		☐	☐	☐	☐	(1)
	Sequence: retells in structural order		☐	☐	☐	☐	(1)
Resolution							
	Name problem solution for the goal		☐	☐	☐	☐	(.5)
	End of the story		☐	☐	☐	☐	(.5)

TOTAL ____ ____ ____ ____

Quantification of Retelling for Narrative Text

Student's Name: <u>Troy</u>

Book/Page: _____ Date: _____

Directions: Place a 1 next to each item the student includes in their retelling. Credit the gist, as well as the obvious recall. Place an * if you ask the child questions to aid recall.

		Level				
		A	B	C	D	
Story sense						
Theme:	Main idea or moral of story	☒	☐	☐	☐	(1)
Problem:	Difficulty to overcome	☐	☐	☐	☐	(1)
Goal:	What the character wants to happen	☐	☐	☐	☐	(1)
Title:	Name of the story (if possible)	☐	☐	☐	☐	(1)
Setting						
	When and where the story occurs	☐	☐	☐	☐	(1)
Characters						
	Name the main characters	☐	☐	☐	☐	(1)
Events/episodes						
	Initiating event	☒	☐	☐	☐	(1)
	Major events (climax)	☐	☐	☐	☐	(1)
	Sequence: retells in structural order	☐	☐	☐	☐	(1)
Resolution						
	Name problem solution for the goal	☐	☐	☐	☐	(.5)
	End the story	☐	☐	☐	☐	(.5)

TOTAL <u>2</u> ___ ___ ___

Comment: Troy only earned 2 points at Level A. Therefore, he should next be provided with Level B (nonprompted retelll with passage).

Case Descriptions: Expository Retell

Joseph was a fourth-grade student in a general education classroom. He was selected by his teacher as an average-performing student in her classroom. Nathan was a fourth-grade student in the same general education classroom as Joseph. His teacher selected him as a student having significant problems in reading in her class. Both students were asked to read the following passage and then to retell the story in their own words, without use of the passage (Level A retell). After reading each student's retell, readers are invited to complete the Quantification of Retelling for Expository Text form provided for each one (see Exercise 3 and Exercise 4). A completed form is provided on the following page in each case, with each student's correct responses denoted by shading.

Passage Read

Flamingos are large, pink-colored wading birds. Some may be 5 feet tall! They have very long, thin necks. They have very long, thin legs, too. They look as if they are walking on stilts. Their feet are webbed like a duck's feet. Flamingos can swim, and they can fly.

Flamingos are birds that live in the warm parts of the world. Some live in Florida in the United States. There are six different kinds of flamingos in the world. They live near salty lakes and rivers.

Flamingos are funny birds to watch. When a flamingo sleeps, it often stands on one leg. It tucks the other leg up under its wing. They often twist their necks around so they can lay their heads on their backs. Another funny thing about flamingos is their knees. Unlike our knees, flamingos' knees bend backward.

Flamingos are good parents. They build nests in mud. The male and female build the nest together. They use their beaks to push mud into the shape of a volcano about 12 inches high. They also use small stones and feathers. It may take some pairs 6 weeks to make their nest!

They usually hatch only one egg at a time. Both the mother and father bird take turns sitting on the egg. When a flamingo baby gets hungry, it squawks. Both parents feed the baby. Flamingo parents feed babies a bright red liquid from their beaks. This liquid is called "crop milk." It is very high in fat and protein. It is produced by both the male and female birds in the upper digestive tract.

Flamingos live together in groups. A group of flamingos is called a *flock* or *colony*. Sometimes they live in colonies of over a million birds.

Results of Retelling for Joseph

Rates: Words correct/minute = 99
Words incorrect/minute = 2

Verbatim transcript: "Umm, they tell you what color they are that, umm, they're how tall they are—they're 5 feet . . . umm . . . that they have very long necks like—like a giraffe but it's kind of short a little . . . umm they have very thin legs also . . . Umm . . . that they live in mud habitats with their babies, and the male and the female take turns sitting on the fla—umm—ah, on the baby flamingo like in its egg . . . umm . . . when the flamingo baby gets hungry it, like, squawks or something, and it like gives like a signal. Flamingos can swim and they can fly . . . umm . . . when they sleep they turn their necks all around, lay them on their back, and they lay on one leg, and they, umm, don't hatch all at one time. They hatch one at a time, and they live together in groups called a *flock* or a *colony*, and they live in the warm parts of the world like Florida or the United States . . . umm . . . there are six different kinds of flamingos in the world. They live near salty lakes and rivers."

Instructions: On Exercise 3 (p. 59), score Joseph's retelling before looking at the scoring form on page 60.

Quantification of Retelling for Expository Text

Student's Name: _____

Title of Passage: _____ Date: _____

Instructions:

- Listen to the child's retell up to two times, while referring to the template provided.
- Circle **1** if the child included the item in their retell, and circle **0** if they omitted the item.
- For the "Topic" and "Main Idea" categories, circle **0** if they omitted the item or part of the item listed on the template, and circle **1** if they completely stated the item listed on the template.
- For "Primary Supporting Details" and "Secondary Supporting Details," circle **0** if they omitted the item, **1** if they provided **1** response, **2** if they provided **2** responses, **3** if they provided **3** responses, and **4** if they provided **4 or more** responses.
- Write the "Total Score" on the line provided (**0–10 points**).

Topic: • Flamingos	0 1
Main idea: • Interesting facts/information about flamingos or flamingos are birds	0 1
Primary supporting details: • Flamingos are large, pink-colored wading birds. • They live in the warm parts of the world. • They usually hatch only one egg at a time. • Both the mother and father bird take turns sitting on the egg. • Both parents make the nest. • Both parents feed the baby. • Flamingo parents feed babies a bright red liquid from their beaks. • Flamingos live together in groups/a group of flamingos is called a *flock* or *colony*. • Flamingos can swim, and they can fly.	0 1 2 3 4
Secondary supporting details: • Some may be 5 feet tall. • They have very long, thin necks. • They have very long, thin legs/they look like they are walking on stilts. • Their feet are webbed like a duck's feet. • Some live in Florida in the United States. • They live near salty lakes and rivers. • When a flamingo sleeps, it often stands on one leg. It tucks the other leg up. • They often twist their necks around so they can lay their heads on their backs. • Flamingos' knees bend backward. • Flamingo parents use their beaks to push mud into the shape of a volcano about 12 inches high/they also use small stones and feathers. • When a flamingo baby gets hungry, it squawks. • "Crop milk" is very high in fat and protein. • Sometimes they live in colonies of over a million birds.	0 1 2 3 4

TOTAL SCORE: _____

Quantification of Retelling for Expository Text

Student's Name: _Joseph_

Title of Passage: _Flamingos_   Date: _____

Instructions:

- Listen to the child's retell up to two times, while referring to the template provided.
- Circle **1** if the child included the item in their retell, and circle **0** if they omitted the item.
- For the "Topic" and "Main Idea" categories, circle **0** if they omitted the item or part of the item listed on the template, and circle **1** if they completely stated the item listed on the template.
- For "Primary Supporting Details" and "Secondary Supporting Details," circle **0** if they omitted the item, **1** if they provided **1** response, **2** if they provided **2** responses, **3** if they provided **3** responses, and **4** if they provided **4 or more** responses.
- Write the "Total Score" on the line provided (**0–10 points**).

Topic: • Flamingos	0 ①
Main idea: • Interesting facts/information about flamingos or flamingos are birds	⓪ 1
Primary supporting details: • Flamingos are large, pink-colored wading birds. • They live in the warm parts of the world. • They usually hatch only one egg at a time. • Both the mother and father bird take turns sitting on the egg. • Both parents make the nest. • Both parents feed the baby. • Flamingo parents feed babies a bright red liquid from their beaks. • Flamingos live together in groups/a group of flamingos is called a _flock_ or _colony_. • Flamingos can swim, and they can fly.	0 1 2 3 ④
Secondary supporting details: • Some may be 5 feet tall. • They have very long, thin necks. • They have very long, thin legs/they look like they are walking on stilts. • Their feet are webbed like a duck's feet. • Some live in Florida in the United States. • They live near salty lakes and rivers. • When a flamingo sleeps, it often stands on one leg. It tucks the other leg up. • They often twist their necks around so they can lay their heads on their backs. • Flamingos' knees bend backward. • Flamingo parents use their beaks to push mud into the shape of a volcano about 12 inches high/they also use small stones and feathers. • When a flamingo baby gets hungry, it squawks. • "Crop milk" is very high in fat and protein. • Sometimes they live in colonies of over a million birds.	0 1 2 3 ④

TOTAL SCORE: _9_

Results of Retelling for Nathan

Rates: Words correct/minute = 34
           Words incorrect/minute = 3

Verbatim transcript: "About flaming—it was about flaming—flaming—flaming—flamingos and about funny things that they can do and they're pink-colored one—one—one—one—one . . . umm . . . they build nets in mud the male and female build the nets together. They use their beaks."

Instructions: On Exercise 4 (p. 62), score Nathan's retelling before looking at the scoring from page 63.

Quantification of Retelling for Expository Text

Student's Name: _____

Title of Passage: _____ Date: _____

Instructions:

- Listen to the child's retell up to two times, while referring to the template provided.
- Circle **1** if the child included the item in their retell, and circle **0** if they omitted the item.
- For the "Topic" and "Main Idea" categories, circle **0** if they omitted the item or part of the item listed on the template, and circle **1** if they completely stated the item listed on the template.
- For "Primary Supporting Details" and "Secondary Supporting Details," circle **0** if they omitted the item, **1** if they provided **1** response, **2** if they provided **2** responses, **3** if they provided **3** responses, and **4** if they provided **4 or more** responses.
- Write the "Total Score" on the line provided (**0–10 points**).

Topic: • Flamingos	0 1
Main idea: • Interesting facts/information about flamingos or flamingos are birds	0 1
Primary supporting details: • Flamingos are large, pink-colored wading birds. • They live in the warm parts of the world. • They usually hatch only one egg at a time. • Both the mother and father bird take turns sitting on the egg. • Both parents make the nest. • Both parents feed the baby. • Flamingo parents feed babies a bright red liquid from their beaks. • Flamingos live together in groups/a group of flamingos is called a *flock* or *colony*. • Flamingos can swim, and they can fly.	0 1 2 3 4
Secondary supporting details: • Some may be 5 feet tall. • They have very long, thin necks. • They have very long, thin legs/they look like they are walking on stilts. • Their feet are webbed like a duck's feet. • Some live in Florida in the United States. • They live near salty lakes and rivers. • When a flamingo sleeps, it often stands on one leg. It tucks the other leg up. • They often twist their necks around so they can lay their heads on their backs. • Flamingos' knees bend backward. • Flamingo parents use their beaks to push mud into the shape of a volcano about 12 inches high/they also use small stones and feathers. • When a flamingo baby gets hungry, it squawks. • "Crop milk" is very high in fat and protein. • Sometimes they live in colonies of over a million birds.	0 1 2 3 4

TOTAL SCORE: _____

Quantification of Retelling for Expository Text

Student's Name: Nathan _____

Title of Passage: Flamingos _____ Date: _____

Instructions:
- Listen to the child's retell up to two times, while referring to the template provided.
- Circle **1** if the child included the item in their retell, and circle **0** if they omitted the item.
- For the "Topic" and "Main Idea" categories, circle **0** if they omitted the item or part of the item listed on the template, and circle **1** if they completely stated the item listed on the template.
- For "Primary Supporting Details" and "Secondary Supporting Details," circle **0** if they omitted the item, **1** if they provided **1** response, **2** if they provided **2** responses, **3** if they provided **3** responses, and **4** if they provided **4 or more** responses.
- Write the "Total Score" on the line provided (**0–10 points**).

Topic: • Flamingos	0 ①
Main idea: • Interesting facts/information about flamingos or flamingos are birds	0 1
Primary supporting details: • Flamingos are large, pink-colored wading birds. • They live in the warm parts of the world. • They usually hatch only one egg at a time. • Both the mother and father bird take turns sitting on the egg. • Both parents make the nest. • Both parents feed the baby. • Flamingo parents feed babies a bright red liquid from their beaks. • Flamingos live together in groups/a group of flamingos is called a *flock* or *colony*. • Flamingos can swim, and they can fly.	0 1 ② 3 4
Secondary supporting details: • Some may be 5 feet tall. • They have very long, thin necks. • They have very long, thin legs/they look like they are walking on stilts. • Their feet are webbed like a duck's feet. • Some live in Florida in the United States. • They live near salty lakes and rivers. • When a flamingo sleeps, it often stands on one leg. It tucks the other leg up. • They often twist their necks around so they can lay their heads on their backs. • Flamingos' knees bend backward. • Flamingo parents use their beaks to push mud into the shape of a volcano about 12 inches high/they also use small stones and feathers. • When a flamingo baby gets hungry, it squawks. • "Crop milk" is very high in fat and protein. • Sometimes they live in colonies of over a million birds.	0 ① 2 3 4

TOTAL SCORE: ___4___

Math

One of the aspects of curriculum-based assessment of math is using *digits correct per minute* or *total digits* as a metric in the scoring of student performance. In addition, to develop more effective interventions, examiners need to be able to conduct an analysis of the types of errors students are making as they complete the math probes. This section of the workbook provides descriptions of how to score math probes using digits correct per minute, along with examples of conducting an analysis of errors. Practice exercises for both scoring and interpretation of math probes are included.

A second component to curriculum-based assessment of math is the evaluation of student performance on measures of mathematical concepts–applications. Scoring these types of measures is not complex; however, developing these types of measures can be time-consuming. An example of this type of measure, along with its scoring, is provided, with indications where readers can obtain commercial measures of mathematics concepts–applications.

USING DIGITS CORRECT IN SCORING MATH PROBES

Typically, when a student is asked to complete math problems, the teacher marks the student's response as either correct or incorrect. Even small and minor errors in the computation process result in the student's obtaining an incorrect answer. In assessing the outcomes of an instructional process, an examiner needs to use a metric that can be sensitive across time to the student's gradual acquisition of the skills required to complete computations accurately. Using the metric of *digits correct* rather than *problems correct* accomplishes this goal.

For example, a student asked to add two three-digit numbers may initially get 0 digits correct:

(1)
$$
\begin{array}{r}
356 \\
+\,678 \\
\hline
922
\end{array}
$$

Recognizing the student's lack of knowledge of regrouping principles, the teacher begins to teach the student how to regroup from the 1's to the 10's column. After some instruction, the student now does the following when given a similar type of problem:

(2)
$$
\begin{array}{r}
467 \\
+\ 589 \\
\hline
946
\end{array}
$$

In this problem, the student only gets one digit correct. After additional instruction, the student produces the results of problem (3):

(3)
$$
\begin{array}{r}
378 \\
+\ 657 \\
\hline
1035
\end{array}
$$

The metric of digits correct makes evident the student's gradual acquisition of the regrouping concept. If the evaluator were to use only the problem's correctness or incorrectness to determine whether the student was learning the concept of regrouping, the student's gradual acquisition of the skill would not be evident—nor would the student receive the gradual reinforcement that encourages further effort.

SCORING DIGITS CORRECT FOR ADDITION AND SUBTRACTION PROBLEMS

The calculation of digits correct when the student is completing addition or subtraction problems is fairly straightforward. Each correct digit <u>below</u> the answer line is counted. If the problem involves regrouping, and the student places numbers above the columns to indicate how much was carried to the next column, these numbers are not counted in the digits-correct figure.

Examples:

$$
\begin{array}{r}
12 \\
+\ 4 \\
\hline
16
\end{array}
$$ (2 digits correct) $$
\begin{array}{r}
145 \\
+\ 672 \\
\hline
817
\end{array}
$$ (3 digits correct)

$$
\begin{array}{r}
54 \\
-\ 27 \\
\hline
27
\end{array}
$$ (2 digits correct) $$
\begin{array}{r}
2{,}675 \\
-\ 1{,}089 \\
\hline
1{,}586
\end{array}
$$ (4 digits correct)

In a math curriculum-based assessment, sets of problems are administered under timed conditions, and a calculation is made of the number of digits correct per minute. Exercise 5 provides an opportunity to practice scoring addition and subtraction math problems using digits correct per minute.

Digits Correct for Addition and Subtraction Problems

Addition and Subtraction Facts with Regrouping to 10's Column

A	B	C	D	E
15 − 9 —— 6	4 − 0 —— 4	76 + 17 —— 81	12 − 8 —— 4	1 + 8 —— 9
F	**G**	**H**	**I**	**J**
8 + 3 —— 11	76 + 6 —— 82	80 − 4 —— 84	47 − 38 —— 11	10 − 5 —— 5
K	**L**	**M**	**N**	**O**
2 + 8 —— 10	0 + 6 —— 6	57 − 9 —— 52	431 − 31 —— 400	15 + 66 —— 81

Scoring: Write in the number of digits correct and incorrect for each problem.

Problem	Digits Correct	Digits Incorrect
A		
B		
C		
D		
E		
F		
G		
H		
I		
J		
K		
L		
M		
N		
O		

Answer Key to Exercise 5

Problem	Digits Correct	Digits Incorrect
A	1	0
B	1	0
C	0	2
D	1	0
E	1	0
F	2	0
G	2	0
H	0	2
I	0	2
J	1	0
K	2	0
L	1	0
M	0	2
N	3	0
O	2	0

Comments

The results of this math probe show several things. First, the digits-correct data place the student within the instructional level for students working within second-grade materials. However, the digits-incorrect results show that the student is making too many errors to be considered instructional. Therefore, the outcome of the probe would demonstrate that the student is in the frustrational level for second-grade material. A careful examination of the probe, however, shows specifically the type of skills that the student has yet to learn. The results show that the student knows basic addition and subtraction facts. However, whenever faced with a problem in which regrouping was required, the student instead subtracted the lower from higher number. The probe suggests that the student has not yet acquired the knowledge of how to regroup in subtraction. Interestingly, the results of problems G and O indicate that the difficulties in regrouping may be specific to subtraction.

Make Up Your Own Addition and Subtraction Problem Exercise Here

A	B	C	D	E
F	G	H	I	J
K	L	M	N	O

Scoring: Write in the number of digits correct and incorrect for each problem.

Problem	Digits Correct	Digits Incorrect
A		
B		
C		
D		
E		
F		
G		
H		
I		
J		
K		
L		
M		
N		
O		

SCORING DIGITS CORRECT FOR MULTIPLICATION PROBLEMS

When multiplication is the skill assessed, counting digits correct can become more complicated. If the problem involves double-digit multiplication, then several digits are usually written below the answer line prior to reaching the final response. Because double-digit multiplication involves the operations of both multiplication and addition, a student could potentially make errors in two types of problems; that is, a student could multiply correctly but add incorrectly, thus getting the wrong answer. Likewise, a student could multiply incorrectly but add correctly, again reaching the wrong answer. If the student were to receive credit only for both multiplying *and* adding correctly, they would be penalized unduly for performing only one incorrect operation. Given that these metrics need to be sensitive to change over time, this would be inappropriate.

As a general rule of thumb, when the metric of digits correct is used in scoring multiplication, a student is given credit for the digit if the operation was performed correctly even if the answer itself is incorrect. For example, if a student asked to multiply a two-digit by two-digit problem did the following:

$$
\begin{array}{r}
75 \\
\times\ 26 \\
\hline
450 \\
\underline{150} \\
2850
\end{array}
$$

the problem would be scored by counting all digits correct below the answer line. There are a total of nine digits correct (indicated in bold) and two incorrect. Seven of the correct digits are the numbers 450 and 150(0), the last 0 being a placeholder, and two digits are correct in the final answer. Thus, this student multiplied correctly but added incorrectly. The score suggests that the difficulties were in the addition portion of the problem since the majority of digits would be scored for multiplication rather than addition.

In contrast, another student performing the same problem may have done the following:

$$
\begin{array}{r}
75 \\
\times\ 26 \\
\hline
435 \\
\underline{285} \\
3415
\end{array}
$$

This problem would be scored as having four digits correct (shown in bold): one digit (the 0 placeholder) under the 1's column under the answer line, plus the three digits showing correct multiplication and addition. In this case, the student multiplied mostly incorrectly and added only partially correctly. Again, counting all digits except the placeholder incorrect would penalize the student unduly, when the real difficulty only lies in multiplication—not in addition or in understanding the correct method for setting up a double-digit multiplication problem.

Exercise 6 is provided for the reader to practice scoring two- and three-digit multiplication problems.

Digits Correct for Two- and Three-Digit Multiplication Problems

A	B	C	D	E
11 × 13 ‾‾‾ 13 11_ ‾‾‾ 123	83 × 48 ‾‾‾ 644 127_ ‾‾‾ 1914	27 × 34 ‾‾‾ 108 81_ ‾‾‾ 918	756 × 8 ‾‾‾ 5648	113 × 59 ‾‾‾ 1017 668_ ‾‾‾ 7697
F	**G**	**H**	**I**	**J**
550 × 66 ‾‾‾ 3300 1216_ ‾‾‾ 15460	186 × 59 ‾‾‾ 1676 4530 ‾‾‾ 6106	536 × 91 ‾‾‾ 536 4824_ ‾‾‾ 48776	710 × 92 ‾‾‾ 1420 6390_ ‾‾‾ 65320	284 × 67 ‾‾‾ 1988 1704_ ‾‾‾ 19028

Scoring: Write in the number of digits correct and incorrect for each problem.

Problem	Digits Correct	Digits Incorrect
A		
B		
C		
D		
E		
F		
G		
H		
I		
J		

Answer Key to Exercise 6:

Problem	Digits Correct	Digits Incorrect
A	7	1
B	7	4
C	9	0
D	2	2
E	10	2
F	10	4
G	7	5
H	13	0
I	14	0
J	14	0

Comments

The results of this probe show that the student, in general, understands the procedure for conducting two- and three-digit multiplication. Errors in place value or setup of the problems are not evident. However, the student does make the mistake in operations when the second digit is supposed to be multiplied. On problems B and F, for example, the student added instead of multiplied. On problem G, the student erred in place values, which resulted in many errors. Finally, it is important to remember to give the student credit for leaving a blank (zero placeholder) in the appropriate columns in most problems. It should also be noted that when the student multiplied incorrectly, they sometimes added correctly. Thus, credit is given for the student's completion of the operation correctly.

Make Up Your Own Multiplication Problem Exercise Here

A	B	C	D	E
F	G	H	I	J

Scoring: Write in the number of digits correct and incorrect for each problem.

Problem	Digits Correct	Digits Incorrect
A		
B		
C		
D		
E		
F		
G		
H		
I		
J		
K		
L		
M		
N		
O		

SCORING DIGITS CORRECT FOR DIVISION PROBLEMS

Division creates several unique problems in the scoring of digits correct and incorrect. Division involving two or more digits requires that students perform three operations: division, multiplication, and subtraction. If one tries to use the digits correct and incorrect metric, it quickly becomes very complex to accurately score these problems. As with multiple-digit multiplication, the rule of thumb for scoring digits correct for division is that digits are counted as correct if the operation is performed correctly and the correct place value is used. For example, in the following example, the student begins the long division problem correctly. (The student's work is shown on the left, the problem done entirely correctly is shown on the right.)

```
        283                      296
   25)7375                  25)7375
        50                       50
       237                      237
       200                      225
        75                      125
        50                      125
        25                        0
```

The student begins by dividing correctly (i.e., 73/25 = 2) and then multiplies correctly (i.e., 2 × 25 = 50). They place the 50 under the correct columns and subtract correctly (i.e., 73 – 50 = 23), and carry down the 7 from the next column. No errors have been made so far. They then make an error in division (i.e., 237/25 = 8) but do multiply correctly (i.e., 25 × 8 = 200). They next make an error in subtraction (i.e., 237 – 200 = 7) and carry down the 5 from the next column. They divide correctly but multiply incorrectly (i.e., 25 × 3 = 50). Finally, they subtract correctly. The student is unsure what to do with the remainder, which, of course, is incorrect in the problem. In this problem, using the rule that correct operations are counted as correct digits, the student scores 14 digits correct (see the items in bold) and 3 incorrect. Looking at the type of errors provides clues as to the student's difficulties (in this case, they erred in basic division), but the scoring of the problem became complex because many of the digits derived by the student did not match the correct solution to the problem. Furthermore, once the error in division was made, the remainder of the problem was incorrect.

A modification to the scoring procedure can reduce the problems that emerge in long division when using the rule of counting correct operations as correct. One simply compares the student's long division to a correct model of long division. The number of digits correct is summed, and a percentage of correct digits out of the total digits possible for the problem is calculated.

The same example is presented below, with the student's work on the left and the model of the correct answer on the right. However, the scoring procedure used here is the percentage of correct digits. Only those digits that are in the correct place and with the correct value are counted.

```
        283                    296
   25)7375                25)7375
      50                     50
      237                    237
      200                    225
       75                    125
       50                    125
       25                      0
```

In the example, the student is given credit for the initial correct division (i.e., 73/25 = 2) and multiplication (i.e., 25 × 2 = 50). The student subtracted correctly (i.e., 73 – 50 = 23), brought the correct number down to the next column, but began to make errors when they divided incorrectly (i.e., 237/25 = 8). From this point forward, the only digits that were counted as correct were the 2 and 5, which were correct compared to the model. The total number of digits that was possible in the problem was 18 (17 digits plus a zero remainder; if a student did not write the zero, they would be given credit for an implied digit). This student got 8 of 18 digits correct, or 44.4% of the total possible digits correct. It is strongly suggested that this method of scoring long division be used.

Exercise 7 provides opportunities to practice scoring division problems for digits correct using the method of matching the student's performance against a correct model.

Digits Correct for Division Problems Using the Match-to-Model Method (Correct Digits in Sample in Boldface)

A	B	C	D	E
50 R3 14)703 **70** 3	**1410 R2** 3)452 **3** **15** 12 32 30 2	**10 R4** 88)884 **88** **04** 0 4	440 22)9950 88 **1150** 880 70	303 29)8787 87 **8** **0** **87** **87** **0**
A—Correct Model 50 R3 14)703 70 *3　3 0　OR 3 *0 in this position is implicit and counted as a digit correct.	**B**—Correct Model 150 R2 3)452 3 15 15 *2　2 0　OR 2 *0 in this position is implicit and counted as a digit correct.	**C**—Correct Model 10 R4 88)884 88 *4　4 0　OR 4 *0 in this position is implicit and counted as a digit correct.	**D**—Correct Model 452 R6 22)9950 88 115 110 50 44 6	**E**—Correct Model 303 29)8787 87 *8　OR　87 0　　　87 87　　　0 87 0** *0 in this position is implicit and counted as a digit correct. **0 remainder is implicit and counted as a digit correct.

Answer Key to Exercise 7:

Problem	Actual Digits Correct	Possible Correct
A	8	8
B	5	12
C	8	8
D	6	16
E	13	13

Comments

Notice that when a remainder is present, the student is given credit for either indicating a remainder in the answer (e.g., writing "R2" in the answer) or leaving the remainder under the last subtraction. They are not given credit for both. The student is not given additional credit for remainders of 0. However, they are given credit for implied 0 digits. For example, in problem C, the student actually wrote in the 0 digit when subtracting 88 – 88. In problem A, the student did not actually write down the 0 when they subtracted 70 – 70; however, this digit was counted in the number of digits correct and possible for the problem. In addition, when student used appropriate shortcuts, they were credited for all digits to solve the problem, as if they had not used shortcuts. Examples A, B, C, and E illustrate the use of a shortcut and the full model for completing the problem.

Make Up Your Own Division Problem Exercise Here

A	B	C	D	E
F	G	H	I	J
K	L	M	N	O

Scoring: Write in the number of digits correct and incorrect for each problem.

Problem	Digits Correct	Digits Incorrect
A		
B		
C		
D		
E		
F		
G		
H		
I		
J		
K		
L		
M		
N		
O		

MATH CONCEPTS–APPLICATIONS

A curriculum-based assessment (CBA) of mathematics needs to go beyond math computation. Determining the ability of children to engage in problem solving, to apply mathematical principles to problems in geometry, time, money, measurement, graphing, numeration, and other such skills, is crucial to fully identifying targets for potential intervention. Assessing student performance across time in these skills provides strong opportunities for linking the assessment and instructional process.

Several commercial products are available to help evaluators conduct a CBA for math concepts–applications. For example, Schoolhouse Technologies (*www. school-housetech.com*) offers sets of worksheets that cover almost every area of mathematics. These worksheets contain single-skill problems that allow in-depth assessment of each area of math applications. Products available from *www.edhelper.com* and *aplusmath.com* allow users to build their own mixed-skills worksheet. AIMSweb® also offers a set of concepts–applications probes for purchase.

Another product that has been found to be very user friendly is available from PRO-ED, Inc. (*www.proedinc.com*). Developed and revised by L. S. Fuchs, Hamlett, and Fuchs (1999) as part of a computerized progress monitoring system, a set of Concepts and Applications probes contains 30 mixed-skills worksheets each for grades 2–8. Each probe contains problems involving measurement, quantity and equivalence concepts, reading charts and graphs, money, time, and solving word problems. The worksheets are scored by summing the number of correct answers that a student attains and dividing by the total number of possible correct problems. Similar Concepts and Applications probe sets (see Figure 8) are now offered by Acadience Learning (*acadiencelearning.org*).

13. One day Jay found 59 cans. The next day he found 19 cans. The day after that he found 16. How many cans did Jay find altogether? _____ cans.

14. What is the area of the rectangle?

_____ units²

15. There are 3 kids. Each kid has 2 red hats and 6 blue hats. How many hats is that in total?

$3 \times (6 + 2) =$ _____

16. Josh starts his swim at 7:45 a.m. He swims for 1 hour 15 minutes. What time does he finish?_____ a.m.

| | | | | | | | | |
|7:30|7:45|8:00|8:15|8:30|8:45|9:00|9:15|9:30|

17. Solve:

$4 \times 4 \times 7 =$ _____

18. Sophie saw a sign on her way to school.
    What is the perimeter of the sign?
    _____ inches.

← 19 inches →

YIELD

19 inches

FIGURE 8. Example of a concepts–application probe for grade 3. Copyright © 2019 Acadience Learning, Inc. Reprinted by permission.

Spelling

USING CORRECT LETTER SEQUENCES IN SCORING SPELLING

As we have just seen, an examiner provides students with partial credit for responses in math using the digits correct metric rather than simply problems correct. An analogous metric exists for spelling: *correct letter sequences*. By counting the number of correct consecutive letters rather than just the words spelled completely correctly, the examiner can detect small improvements in a student's responses. In addition, the types of errors made can be diagnostic; they can help the examiner identify the skills that a student has mastered and the ones that need to be targeted in future interventions.

SCORING CORRECT LETTER SEQUENCES

- **Step 1.** The examiner places a blank before the first and last letter of each word to be scored. The blank is considered as a correct phantom character and is used to enable the initial and ending letters of words to be counted. For example:

$$\_ s\ a\ m\ p\ l\ e \_$$

- **Step 2.** A linking symbol (⌒) is used to connect each letter to the next, beginning with the initial blank before the first letter. These should be placed alternately above and below consecutive letters:

$$\_⌒s\_a⌒m\_p⌒l\_e⌒\_$$

- **Step 3.** The examiner counts the number of letter sequences that are correct. The word *sample* above has a total of seven possible correct letter sequences.

Special Scoring Situations

Certain words create a need for special rules and conventions. In particular, the presence of double consonants can be confusing when using the letter sequences metric. If the student omits one of the consonants, credit is given only once. By comparing the student's spelling with the correct spelling, this can become evident. For example, the word

$$\_\,\widehat{\ }b\_u\widehat{\ }b\_b\widehat{\ }l\_e\widehat{\ }\_$$

contains a total of seven possible letter sequences. A student who spells the word as

$$\_\,\widehat{\ }b\_u\widehat{\ }b\_l\widehat{\ }e\_$$

would be scored as having five letter sequences correct. The *b* to start the word is correct, therefore, points are awarded for the connections between the placeholder at the start of the word and *b*. Additional points are awarded for the connections between *b* and *u* and *u* and *b*. The lack of the second *b* results in an incorrect sequence (no connection of *b* to *l*), but the other remaining sequences, *l* and *e* and *e* and the ending placeholder, are correct.

Exercises 8 and 9, for practicing the scoring of spelling using correct letter sequences, are provided.

Scoring for Letters in Sequence for Spelling

Instructions: Listed below are the actual way in which students spelled words on a weekly spelling test. The correct spelling is provided in the next column. Indicate the number of correct letter sequences for each word. The following page provides an answer sheet.

Word Spelled by Student	Correct Spelling	Letter Sequences Correct/Total Possible	Word Spelled Correctly?
rain	rain		
belong	belong		
botin	button		
slat	salt		
clock	clock		
smart	smart		
stap	step		
shep	sheep		
mint	minute		
above	above		
greup	group		
hunt	hut		
kesz	crazy		
jock	joke		
mire	mirror		
riad	drove		
nose	noise		

Answer Sheet for Exercise 8

Note: The first two words are scored as examples.

Word Spelled by Student	Correct Spelling	Letter Sequences Correct/Total Possible	Word Spelled Correctly?
_ˆr_aˆi_nˆ_	rain	5/5	✓
_ˆb_eˆl_oˆn_gˆ_	belong	7/7	✓
botin	button	2/7	
slat	salt	2/5	
clock	clock	6/6	✓
smart	smart	6/6	✓
stap	step	3/5	
shep	sheep	4/6	
mint	minute	3/7	
above	above	6/6	✓
greup	group	4/6	
hunt	hut	3/4	
kesz	crazy	0/6	
jock	joke	2/5	
mire	mirror	3/7	
riad	drove	0/6	
nose	noise	4/6	

Scoring for Letters in Sequence for Spelling

Instructions: Listed below are the actual way in which students spelled words on a weekly spelling test. The correct spelling is provided in the next column. Indicate the number of correct letter sequences for each word. The following page provides an answer sheet.

Word Spelled by Student	Correct Spelling	Letter Sequences Correct/Total Possible	Word Spelled Correctly?
scad	scold		
srey	sorry		
tow	tall		
hapin	happen		
fi	fourth		
alive	alive		
give	given		
dip	drop		
terth	teeth		
beer	bear		
beck	drink		
sotp	stop		
north	north		
jell	jail		
thre	flower		
leve	leave		
insiad	inside		

Answer Sheet for Exercise 9

Note: The first two words are scored as examples.

Word Spelled by Student	Correct Spelling	Letter Sequences Correct/Total Possible	Word Spelled Correctly?
⌢s⌣c a d⌢_	scold	3/6	
_⌢s r e y⌢_	sorry	2/6	
tow	tall	1/5	
hapin	happen	4/7	
fi	fourth	0/7	
alive	alive	6/6	✓
give	given	4/6	
dip	drop	2/5	
terth	teeth	4/6	
beer	bear	3/5	
beck	drink	0/6	
sotp	stop	2/5	
north	north	6/6	✓
jell	jail	2/5	
thre	flower	0/7	
leve	leave	4/6	
insiad	inside	4/7	

Written Language

Written language assessments collected as part of the assessment of academic skills problems can be scored in multiple ways. Each of these metrics is used for a somewhat different purpose.

SCORING FOR WORDS WRITTEN

The simplest metric is to count the total number of words written. This metric is a strategy commonly used when the purpose of the assessment is progress monitoring. When an evaluator is using this metric, a word is counted if it is separated from other words in the written material. Words are counted regardless of whether they are spelled correctly or are phonetically recognizable. For example, a student given the story starter "When my video game started predicting the future, I knew I had to . . ." wrote the following during a 3-minute period: "got my mom to check it out I was ckerd it was hard to recat but my mom helped me then my brather came in to my room he helped me to but he left my room want down." Notice that many of the words are not recognizable, nor do they make sense in the context of the story as subsequently dictated by the student. The number of words written, however, would be scored as 39.

SCORING FOR WRITING MECHANICS

When the evaluator is more interested in short-term monitoring and the development of effective interventions, strengths and weaknesses in the mechanics of writing need to be assessed. This is most easily accomplished by developing a checklist that can be used repeatedly after each written language assessment is administered. Form 9 provides an example of a quality evaluation measure that one could use for assessing mechanics such as capitalization, punctuation, sentence construction, paragraph construction, and appearance of the written product. Exercise 10 provides a set of written responses from students to practice scoring using all three sets of measures.

Quality Evaluation Measure for Written Products—Elementary Level

Student Name: _____

Date: _____

Grade: _____

Rating Scale:

3 = Skill used consistently and accurately throughout written product (>95% of time)

2 = Skill used frequently and accurately throughout written product (50–94% of time)

1 = Skill used infrequently or inaccurately (<50% of the time)

0 = No evidence of skill

Capitalization

First words in sentences are capitalized		0	1	2	3
Proper nouns are capitalized		0	1	2	3
Capitals are not used improperly		0	1	2	3

Punctuation

Punctuation occurs at the end of each sentence		0	1	2	3
End punctuation is correct		0	1	2	3

Sentence Construction

Absence of run-on sentences		0	1	2	3
Absence of sentence fragments		0	1	2	3
Absence of nonsensical sentences		0	1	2	3

Paragraph Construction

Each paragraph contains a topic sentence	N/A	0	1	2	3
Each sentence within a paragraph relates to the topic sentence	N/A	0	1	2	3

Appearance of Written Product

Words are legible		0	1	2	3
Spacing is appropriate between letters/words		0	1	2	3
Margins are appropriate		0	1	2	3
Written product is neat, with correct spelling		0	1	2	3

TOTAL SCORE ____

From *Academic Skills Problems Fifth Edition Workbook* by Edward S. Shapiro and Nathan H. Clemens. Copyright © 2023 The Guilford Press. Permission to photocopy this form is granted to purchasers of this book for personal use or use with students (see copyright page for details). Purchasers can download additional copies of this form (see the box at the end of the table of contents).

SCORING BRIEF WRITTEN LANGUAGE SAMPLES: EXAMPLES AND EXERCISES

Below are three written samples, collected as 3-minute story starters during a direct assessment of written expression. All students were in the fifth grade. In Exercises 10, 11, and 12, readers can practice using the Quality Evaluation Measure for Written Products—Elementary Level to score the samples. A scored form follows each blank form (all answers are underlined).

Starter and Writing Samples

Starter: "When my video game started predicting the future, I knew I had to . . ."

Student 1: Bryan

> "got my mom to check it out I was ckerd it was hard to recat but my mom holped me then my brother came in to my room he helped my to but he left my room want down."

Student 2: Valesa

> "Get it to put back on my other game and when the future came on my board I was very surprised because it was talking to me and I did not now wat it was talking about and it just kep on talking to me and when it said I was going to live in mars I said y must I live on mars he said because you have to and I said how comes."

Student 3: Cary

> "run and get my camera. I ran into my room to find it, it was gone. I wanted to see what it would do if I turned it off. I put my hand on the power button, and I felt a stinging shock on my finger. I ran to get my mom. By the time she got there, it was too late."

Quality Evaluation Measure for Written Products—Elementary Level

Student Name: _____

Date: _____

Grade: _____

Rating Scale:

    3 =   Skill used consistently and accurately throughout written product (>95% of time)

    2 =   Skill used frequently and accurately throughout written product (50–94% of time)

    1 =   Skill used infrequently or inaccurately (<50% of the time)

    0 =   No evidence of skill

Capitalization

First words in sentences are capitalized	0	1	2	3
Proper nouns are capitalized	0	1	2	3
Capitals are not used improperly	0	1	2	3

Punctuation

Punctuation occurs at the end of each sentence	0	1	2	3
End punctuation is correct	0	1	2	3

Sentence Construction

Absence of run-on sentences	0	1	2	3
Absence of sentence fragments	0	1	2	3
Absence of nonsensical sentences	0	1	2	3

Paragraph Construction

Each paragraph contains a topic sentence	N/A	0	1	2	3
Each sentence within a paragraph relates to the topic sentence	N/A	0	1	2	3

Appearance of Written Product

Words are legible	N/A	0	1	2	3
Spacing is appropriate between letters/words	N/A	0	1	2	3
Margins are appropriate	N/A	0	1	2	3
Written product is neat, with correct spelling	N/A	0	1	2	3

TOTAL SCORE ____

Quality Evaluation Measure for Written Products—Elementary Level

Student Name: Bryan

Date: 4-21-21

Grade: 5

Rating Scale:

    3 = Skill used consistently and accurately throughout written product (>95% of time)

    2 = Skill used frequently and accurately throughout written product (50–94% of time)

    1 = Skill used infrequently or inaccurately (<50% of the time)

    0 = No evidence of skill

Capitalization

First words in sentences are capitalized	<u>0</u>	1	2	3
Proper nouns are capitalized	<u>0</u>	1	2	3
Capitals are not used improperly	<u>0</u>	1	2	3

Punctuation

Punctuation occurs at the end of each sentence	<u>0</u>	1	2	3
End punctuation is correct	<u>0</u>	1	2	3

Sentence Construction

Absence of run-on sentences	<u>0</u>	1	2	3
Absence of sentence fragments	0	<u>1</u>	2	3
Absence of nonsensical sentences	0	1	2	<u>3</u>

Paragraph Construction

Each paragraph contains a topic sentence	<u>N/A</u>	0	1	2	3
Each sentence within a paragraph relates to the topic sentence	<u>N/A</u>	0	1	2	3

Appearance of Written Product

Words are legible	<u>N/A</u>	0	1	2	3
Spacing is appropriate between letters/words	<u>N/A</u>	0	1	2	3
Margins are appropriate	<u>N/A</u>	0	1	2	3
Written product is neat, with correct spelling	<u>N/A</u>	0	1	2	3

TOTAL SCORE 4

Quality Evaluation Measure for Written Products—Elementary Level

Student Name: _____

Date: _____

Grade: _____

Rating Scale:

3 = Skill used consistently and accurately throughout written product (>95% of time)

2 = Skill used frequently and accurately throughout written product (50–94% of time)

1 = Skill used infrequently or inaccurately (<50% of the time)

0 = No evidence of skill

Capitalization

First words in sentences are capitalized		0	1	2	3
Proper nouns are capitalized		0	1	2	3
Capitals are not used improperly		0	1	2	3

Punctuation

Punctuation occurs at the end of each sentence		0	1	2	3
End punctuation is correct		0	1	2	3

Sentence Construction

Absence of run-on sentences		0	1	2	3
Absence of sentence fragments		0	1	2	3
Absence of nonsensical sentences		0	1	2	3

Paragraph Construction

Each paragraph contains a topic sentence	N/A	0	1	2	3
Each sentence within a paragraph relates to the topic sentence	N/A	0	1	2	3

Appearance of Written Product

Words are legible	N/A	0	1	2	3
Spacing is appropriate between letters/words	N/A	0	1	2	3
Margins are appropriate	N/A	0	1	2	3
Written product is neat, with correct spelling	N/A	0	1	2	3

TOTAL SCORE ____

Quality Evaluation Measure for Written Products—Elementary Level

Student Name: _Valesa_

Date: _4-21-21_

Grade: _5_

Rating Scale:

3 = Skill used consistently and accurately throughout written product (>95% of time)

2 = Skill used frequently and accurately throughout written product (50–94% of time)

1 = Skill used infrequently or inaccurately (<50% of the time)

0 = No evidence of skill

Capitalization

First words in sentences are capitalized	0	_1_	2	3
Proper nouns are capitalized	0	1	_2_	3
Capitals are not used improperly	0	1	2	_3_

Punctuation

Punctuation occurs at the end of each sentence	_0_	1	2	3
End punctuation is correct	_0_	1	2	3

Sentence Construction

Absence of run-on sentences	0	1	2	_3_
Absence of sentence fragments	0	1	2	_3_
Absence of nonsensical sentences	0	1	2	_3_

Paragraph Construction

Each paragraph contains a topic sentence	_N/A_	0	1	2	3
Each sentence within a paragraph relates to the topic sentence	_N/A_	0	1	2	3

Appearance of Written Product

Words are legible	_N/A_	0	1	2	3
Spacing is appropriate between letters/words	_N/A_	0	1	2	3
Margins are appropriate	_N/A_	0	1	2	3
Written product is neat, with correct spelling	_N/A_	0	1	2	3

TOTAL SCORE _15_

Quality Evaluation Measure for Written Products—Elementary Level

Student Name: _____

Date: _____

Grade: _____

Rating Scale:

    3 =   Skill used consistently and accurately throughout written product (>95% of time)

    2 =   Skill used frequently and accurately throughout written product (50–94% of time)

    1 =   Skill used infrequently or inaccurately (<50% of the time)

    0 =   No evidence of skill

Capitalization

First words in sentences are capitalized	0	1	2	3
Proper nouns are capitalized	0	1	2	3
Capitals are not used improperly	0	1	2	3

Punctuation

Punctuation occurs at the end of each sentence	0	1	2	3
End punctuation is correct	0	1	2	3

Sentence Construction

Absence of run-on sentences	0	1	2	3
Absence of sentence fragments	0	1	2	3
Absence of nonsensical sentences	0	1	2	3

Paragraph Construction

Each paragraph contains a topic sentence	N/A	0	1	2	3
Each sentence within a paragraph relates to the topic sentence	N/A	0	1	2	3

Appearance of Written Product

Words are legible	N/A	0	1	2	3
Spacing is appropriate between letters/words	N/A	0	1	2	3
Margins are appropriate	N/A	0	1	2	3
Written product is neat, with correct spelling	N/A	0	1	2	3

TOTAL SCORE ____

Quality Evaluation Measure for Written Products—Elementary Level

Student Name: _Cary_

Date: _4-21-21_

Grade: _5_

Rating Scale:

 3 = Skill used consistently and accurately throughout written product (>95% of time)

 2 = Skill used frequently and accurately throughout written product (50–94% of time)

 1 = Skill used infrequently or inaccurately (<50% of the time)

 0 = No evidence of skill

Capitalization

First words in sentences are capitalized	0	1	2	_3_
Proper nouns are capitalized	0	1	2	_3_
Capitals are not used improperly	0	1	2	_3_

Punctuation

Punctuation occurs at the end of each sentence	0	1	2	_3_
End punctuation is correct	0	1	2	_3_

Sentence Construction

Absence of run-on sentences	0	1	2	_3_
Absence of sentence fragments	0	1	2	_3_
Absence of nonsensical sentences	0	1	2	_3_

Paragraph Construction

Each paragraph contains a topic sentence	_N/A_	0	1	2	3
Each sentence within a paragraph relates to the topic sentence	_N/A_	0	1	2	3

Appearance of Written Product

Words are legible	_N/A_	0	1	2	3
Spacing is appropriate between letters/words	_N/A_	0	1	2	3
Margins are appropriate	_N/A_	0	1	2	3
Written product is neat, with correct spelling	_N/A_	0	1	2	3

TOTAL SCORE _24_

ASSESSING WRITING QUALITY OF LONGER WRITING SAMPLES

The evaluator may also be interested in the overall quality of the student's writing, particularly with regard to aspects of writing quality that are often used to evaluate the written products of older students (i.e., late elementary, middle, and secondary grades). In these situations, rubrics and scales can be used to evaluate longer pieces of writing across multiple dimensions. Troia (2018) developed one such rubric, which is provided in Form 10. Troia's rubric offers the ability to score a student's writing sample on dimensions such as coherence, development of ideas, varied language and vocabulary, and other aspects that define writing quality.

FORM 10

Writing Scoring Rubric

Scoring dimension	No evidence of dimensional quality; severely flawed/difficult to read (0)	Minimal evidence of dimensional quality; substantially flawed/difficult to read (1)	Some evidence of dimensional quality; notably flawed but readable (2)	Adequate evidence of dimensional quality; a few consistent flaws but readable (3)	Strong evidence of dimensional quality; some inconsistent flaws/ easy to read (4)	Excellent evidence of dimensional quality; virtually no flaws/fully comprehensible (5)
Orients the reader to the purpose of the text effectively and creatively						
Groups related ideas to enhance text coherence logically and insightfully						
Provides a concluding sentence or section that follows smoothly from prior ideas						
Links ideas using words or phrases precisely and effectively for strong cohesion						
Develops ideas using facts, examples, experiences, descriptive details, dialogue/quotes (from source materials as appropriate) that are relevant and impactful						
Uses language and vocabulary that are precise, varied, and apt for the type of text						
Is free of errors in grammar, usage, and mechanics (spelling, capitalization, and punctuation)						

TOTAL SCORE = _____

Scoring Procedures:
a) If scoring multiple students' writing samples, separate papers to score into three sets representing low, medium, and high overall quality based on initial impressions prior to using the rubric.
b) Score each of the seven dimensions separately using the 6-point scale above, working in reverse order from last to first dimension.
c) Sum the total points awarded across dimensions to obtain the paper's score (range from 0 to 35).

From Troia (2018). Reprinted by permission in *Academic Skills Problems Fifth Edition Workbook* by Edward S. Shapiro and Nathan H. Clemens (The Guilford Press, 2023). Permission to photocopy this form is granted to purchasers of this book for personal use or use with students (see copyright page for details). Purchasers can download additional copies of this form (see the box at the end of the table of contents).

Summary Form for Academic Assessment

Data obtained during Steps 1 and 2 represent the collection of extensive information about a student's present level of academic performance. The data also provide a means of examining the academic environment in which the student's problems are occurring. To facilitate the process of assembling these data, a form for summarizing these data (Form 11) is provided. The form offers a place to organize data and other information, and provides (1) a holistic sense of the assessment, (2) a way to identify areas of relative strength and weakness, (3) identification of areas of the assessment that may have been missed, and (4) a helpful organization for report writing. We remind readers that this form is used for summary and organization, not as the report itself.

FORM 11

Data Summary Form for Academic Assessment

The purpose of this form is to assist in aggregating and summarizing the data from the academic assessment. Skip any questions or sections that are not relevant or were not assessed. This form is provided to assist the evaluator in decision making and report writing but is not to be used as the report itself.

Child's name: _____

Teacher: _____

Grade: _____

School: _____

School district: _____

Date: _____

Teacher-Reported Primary Area of Concern: _____

Teacher-Reported Secondary Area of Concern: _____

Teacher-Reported Areas of Relative Strength: _____

TEACHER-REPORTED STUDENT BEHAVIOR

Rate the following areas from 1 to 5 (0 = Never, 5 = Always):

a. Stays engaged (on-task) during teacher-led large-group instruction _____

b. Stays engaged (on-task) during teacher-led small-group instruction _____

c. Stays engaged (on-task) during partner work or independent work _____

d. Follows directions _____

e. Shows effort and persistence, even when work is difficult _____

f. Asks for help when needed _____

g. Completes tests or classwork in allotted time _____

h. Completes homework on time _____

i. Engages in behaviors that disrupt instruction or peers' learning _____

Student's behavior is reported to be more problematic in: _____

_____

Summary of Additional Behavior Rating Scale Data (if administered)

Scale: _____

Summary of scores (include subscale scores and total scores, as applicable) and percentile ranks: ____

_____

_____

(continued)

From *Academic Skills Problems Fifth Edition Workbook* by Edward S. Shapiro and Nathan H. Clemens. Copyright © 2023 The Guilford Press. Permission to photocopy this form is granted to purchasers of this book for personal use or use with students (see copyright page for details). Purchasers can download additional copies of this form (see the box at the end of the table of contents).

Behavior notes and additional information: _____

_____

_____

READING—SKILLS

Teacher-Reported Primary Area(s) of Reading Difficulty: _____

Title of curriculum series, materials used for reading instruction: _____

_____

Reading skills expected of student at present grade and time of year: _____

_____

Summary of Direct Assessment Scores of Reading Skills (leave cells blank if not assessed or applicable)

Keystone Skill Area	Test/Measure/Subtest	Raw Score	Correct/Errors (if applicable)	Standard Score	Percentile Rank
Vocabulary, Language Comprehension					
Phonological Awareness					
Alphabetic Knowledge					
Word Reading, Decoding					
Spelling					
Text Reading Efficiency					
Reading Comprehension					

(continued)

If Word Reading/Decoding skills are a concern, what types of words does the student find challenging? _____

_____

What types of words is the student more successful at reading? _____

_____

Reading Survey-Level Assessment: Results of Oral Reading Passages Administered

Grade Level/Book	Passage	Words Correct per Minute	Words Incorrect per Minute	% correct	Median Scores for Level			Learning Level (Independent, Instructional, Frustrational)
					WC	ER	%C	
	1							
	2							
	3							
	1							
	2							
	3							
	1							
	2							
	3							
	1							
	2							
	3							

Summary of review of reading permanent products: _____

_____

_____

READING—ENVIRONMENT

Instructional Procedures:

General nature and focus of reading instruction: _____

_____

Proportion of large-group, small-group, independent work: _____

Number of reading groups: _____

Student's reading group (if applicable): _____

Allotted time/day for reading: _____

Student aware of rules/expectations/routines: ☐ Yes ☐ No

Contingencies: _____

(continued)

Observations: _____ None completed for this area

System used:

- ☐ BOSS
- ☐ Other _____

Setting of observations:

- ☐ ISW:TPsnt   ☐ SmGp:Tled   ☐ Co-op
- ☐ ISW:TSmGp   ☐ LgGp:Tled   ☐ Other _____

BOSS results:

Target_____	Peer _____	Target _____	Peer _____
AET%_____	AET%_____	OFT-M% _____	OFT-M% _____
PET%_____	PET%_____	OFT-V% _____	OFT-V% _____
		OFT-P% _____	OFT-P% _____
	TDI%_____		

Intervention Strategies Previously Attempted:

_____ Simple _____

_____ Moderate _____

_____ Intensive _____

STUDENT INTERVIEW—READING   _____ Not completed for this area

Understands expectations of teacher	Yes	No	Not sure
Understands assignments	Yes	No	Not sure
Feels they can do the assignments	Yes	No	Not sure
Likes the subject	Yes	No	Not sure
Feels they are given enough time to complete assignments	Yes	No	Not sure
Feels as if they are called on to participate in discussions	Yes	No	Not sure
Feels as if they can improve in [referred skill area] with effort and support	Yes	No	Not sure

Reading—Overall Summary Notes: _____

_____

_____

_____

_____

_____

MATHEMATICS—SKILLS

Mathematics curriculum/program used for instruction: _____

Specific problems in mathematics: _____

(continued)

Summary of Direct Assessment Scores of Mathematics Skills (leave cells blank if not assessed or applicable)

Keystone Skill Area	Test/Measure/Subtest	Raw Score	Correct/Errors (if applicable)	Standard Score	Percentile Rank
Early Numerical Competencies					
Number Combinations					
Procedural Computation					
Word-Problem Solving (and/or Pre-Algebraic Reasoning)					
Rational Numbers					
Geometry and Measurement					
Algebra					

Summary of review of mathematics permanent products: _____

_____

_____

_____

MATHEMATICS—ENVIRONMENT

Instructional Procedures:

Allotted time/day: _____

Teaching procedures, how instruction is divided, etc.: _____

_____

Contingencies: _____

(continued)

Observations: _____ None completed for this area

System used:

   ☐ BOSS

   ☐ Other _____

Setting of observations:

   ☐ ISW:TPsnt   ☐ SmGp:Tled   ☐ Co-op

   ☐ ISW:TSmGp   ☐ LgGp:Tled   ☐ Other _____

BOSS results:

Target_____	Peer _____	Target _____	Peer _____
AET%_____	AET%_____	OFT-M% _____	OFT-M% _____
PET%_____	PET%_____	OFT-V% _____	OFT-V% _____
		OFT-P% _____	OFT-P% _____
	TDI%_____		

Mathematics Intervention Strategies Attempted:

_____ Simple _____

_____ Moderate _____

_____ Intensive _____

STUDENT INTERVIEW—MATHEMATICS _____ None completed for this area

Understands expectations of teacher	Yes	No	Not sure
Understands assignments	Yes	No	Not sure
Feels they can do the assignments	Yes	No	Not sure
Likes the subject	Yes	No	Not sure
Feels they are given enough time to complete assignments	Yes	No	Not sure
Feels as if they are called on to participate in discussions	Yes	No	Not sure
Feels as if they can improve in [referred skill area] with effort and support	Yes	No	Not sure

Mathematics—Overall Summary Notes: _____

_____

_____

_____

_____

_____

(continued)

WRITING—SKILLS

Types of writing assignments and expectations for students at present grade and time of year: _____

_____

_____

_____

Summary of Direct Assessment Scores of Writing Skills (leave cells blank if not assessed or applicable)

Keystone Skill Area	Test/Measure/Scale/Subtest (and scoring metric, if applicable)	Score	Standard Score	Percentile Rank
Transcription: Handwriting, Writing Fluency				
Transcription: Spelling				
Grammar, Syntax				
Composition Quality				

Summary of review of writing permanent products: _____

_____

_____

_____

Are low motivation and/or low self-regulation involved in the student's writing difficulties? _____

_____

Are oral language difficulties involved in the student's writing difficulties? _____

_____

_____

(continued)

WRITING—ENVIRONMENT

Instructional Procedures:

Allotted time/day: _____

Teaching procedures, activities: _____

Observations: _____ None completed for this area

System used:

☐ BOSS

☐ Other _____

Setting of observations:

☐ ISW:TPsnt   ☐ SmGp:Tled   ☐ Co-op

☐ ISW:TSmGp   ☐ LgGp:Tled   ☐ Other _____

BOSS results:

Target_____	Peer _____	Target _____	Peer _____
AET%_____	AET%_____	OFT-M% _____	OFT-M% _____
PET%_____	PET%_____	OFT-V% _____	OFT-V% _____
	TDI%_____	OFT-P% _____	OFT-P% _____

School MTSS/RTI Model (complete only if the school has one)

Grade levels and skill areas covered by the model: _____

For how many years has the model been in place?

☐ Less than 1 year   ☐ 1 year   ☐ 2 years   ☐ 3+ years

Is this student assigned to tiered instruction beyond Tier 1?

☐ No   ☐ Yes, skill area(s): _____

To which tier is the student currently assigned?

☐ Tier 1   ☐ Tier 2   ☐ Tier 3   ☐ Other _____

Describe the interventions that have been used for the student (as applicable):

Tier 2 _____

Tier 3 _____

What are the benchmark scores (and measures) for the student in the current year (if available)?

Fall _____

Winter _____

Spring _____

What are the expected benchmark scores (and measures) for the student in the current year (if available)?

Fall _____

Winter _____

Spring _____

(continued)

What is the student's rate of improvement (ROI) for progress monitoring (if available)?

Expected ROI _____

Targeted ROI _____

Attained ROI _____

Hypothesis Development

Primary area of difficulty: _____

Suspected skill deficits that are the reason for the difficulty: _____

_____

Difficulties with behaviors or learning-related skills that may be contributing to the problem: _____

_____

Possible environmental and instructional factors contributing to the problem: _____

_____

Relative strengths (academic or social/behavioral) that may mitigate the problem: _____

_____

Hypothesis Statement Framework. This is meant as a guide to assist hypothesis writing. It should be refined and revised as needed (e.g., relevant aspects added or irrelevant aspects omitted). Separate hypotheses can be written for secondary areas of difficulty.

_____'s difficulties in [reading/mathematics/writing] appear to be due to inadequate or underdeveloped skills in _____. These difficulties appear [or do not appear] to be related to the student's behaviors or learning-related skills, which include _____ _____. The student's difficulties appear [or do not appear] to be related to instructional or classroom environment factors, which may include _____. Compared to their area(s) of difficulty, the student demonstrates relative strengths in _____

_____.

Instructional Modification

Strategies for instructional modification can be conceptualized on a continuum of complexity and the degree to which they require changes to existing programs. As illustrated in Figure 9, strategies are viewed as general/simple, moderate, or specific intensive. The idea is that the strategies selected for a given student need only be as complex and intensive as is necessary. More complex interventions require greater resources and more extensive changes to existing programs and schedules; therefore, more complex strategies should be reserved for situations where simpler approaches are insufficient or ineffective. Given the student's assessment results, combining applicable strategies from across the continuum may be appropriate.

At the level of simple strategies, the focus is improving the clarity of expectations and enhancing student motivation by altering the type of feedback given to student responses, altering the instructional presentation, or presenting other strategies that may impact the way in which the teaching process is proceeding. Two examples of these types of strategies are provided in Forms 12 and 13. Form 12 (regrouping checklist) provides a set of cues for a student to follow as they complete problems of addition and subtraction with regrouping. This simple checklist offers students reminders of the sequential process needed in correctly completing problems of regrouping to the 10's column. Form 13 (reading checklist) is a list of reminders for students to follow when they are struggling with understanding sentences. The checklist offers students an opportunity to manage their own instructional process. Self-monitoring strategies are another approach in this category. As described in Chapter 5 of *Academic Skills Problems, Fifth Edition*, self-monitoring strategies do not require any changes to instruction and can be designed for a wide range of behaviors and any academic area or school activity.

When simple interventions are not sufficient to improve student performance, more moderate levels of interventions can be used. Interventions of moderate intensity involve enhancing existing instruction to make it more explicit, increasing the delivery and consistency of affirmative and corrective feedback, and improving the pace of instruction. Existing instruction can also be improved by adding peer

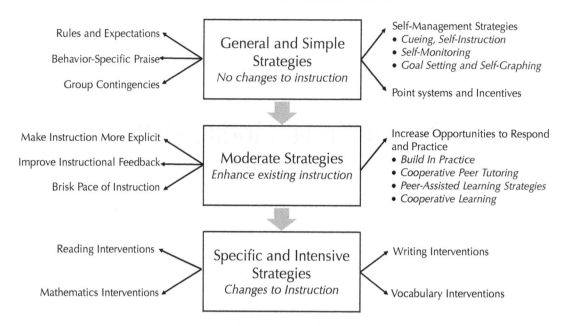

FIGURE 9. Continuum of intensity of instructional modifications and interventions.

tutoring. One of the most effective peer-tutoring techniques is peer-assisted learning strategies© (PALS), developed by Lynn and Doug Fuchs at Vanderbilt University (*kc. vanderbilt.edu/pals*). These strategies have been identified by both the What Works Clearinghouse (*ies.ed.gov/ncee/wwc*) and Best Evidence Encyclopedia (*www.bestevidence.org*) as top-rated programs with strong empirical support.

Many times, neither simple nor moderate levels of intervention result in the desired improvements in student performance. Strategies considered to be intensive may be needed; these often involve changes in instructional grouping, instructional materials, or methods of instruction. Resources that identify available strategies are plentiful. Some key resources that readers will find valuable can be found on websites such as the National Center on Intensive Intervention (*www.intensiveintervention. org*), Intervention Central (*www.interventioncentral.org*), as well as in the practice guides published by the U.S. Department of Education, Institute of Education Sciences (*ies.ed.gov/ncee/wwc/publications/practiceguides*). The practice guides are especially important because the strategies provided in them are based on an evaluation of existing empirical evidence and can point users to the relative strength in research to support the recommended practices. In addition, some excellent print publications that provide intervention descriptions that can be recommended are books by Rathvon (2008; *Effective School Interventions: Evidence-Based Strategies for Improving School Outcomes*) as well as books by Shinn and Walker (2010; *Interventions for Achievement and Behavior Problems in a Three-Tier Model Including RTI*). These are just some of the many excellent resources available to support the selection and development of instructional modification strategies.

Presented here are intervention strategies that have been found to be useful for practice in developing academic skills. The strategies can be applied broadly across skill areas.

FORM 12

Regrouping Checklist for Addition and Subtraction

Is the problem addition or subtraction?

Addition Checklist

☐ Add the 1's column.

☐ Is the answer more than 10?

   ☐ Put the 1's below the answer line.

   ☐ Put a 1 on top of the 10's column.

☐ Add the 10's column.

Subtraction Checklist

☐ Look at the 1's column.

☐ Can I subtract? Is the top number bigger than the bottom number?
If NO:

   ☐ Go to the 10's and take away 1.

   ☐ Add the 10's to the 1's by placing a 1 in front of the top number.

☐ Subtract the 1's.

☐ Subtract the 10's.

From *Academic Skills Problems Fifth Edition Workbook* by Edward S. Shapiro and Nathan H. Clemens. Copyright © 2023 The Guilford Press. Permission to photocopy this form is granted to purchasers of this book for personal use or use with students (see copyright page for details). Purchasers can download additional copies of this form (see the box at the end of the table of contents).

FORM 13

Checklist for Sentence Checking

Sentence Check . . . *"Did I understand this sentence?"*

If you had trouble understanding a word in the sentence, try . . .

☐ Reading the sentence over.

☐ Reading the next sentence.

☐ Looking up the word in the glossary (if the book or article has one).

☐ Asking someone.

If you had trouble understanding the meaning of the sentence, try . . .

☐ Reading the whole paragraph again.

☐ Reading on.

☐ Asking someone.

From *Academic Skills Problems Fifth Edition Workbook* by Edward S. Shapiro and Nathan H. Clemens. Copyright © 2023 The Guilford Press. Permission to photocopy this form is granted to purchasers of this book for personal use or use with students (see copyright page for details). Purchasers can download additional copies of this form (see the box at the end of the table of contents).

The Incremental Rehearsal Technique

The *incremental rehearsal* technique has been found to be a powerful strategy that can be useful in interventions whose objective is for a student to acquire new, fact-based information. The intervention can cut across subjects and may be used for teaching skills such as letter or number recognition, letter–sound correspondence (including the sounds of letter combinations and pronunciation of affixes), word reading, number combinations (i.e., math facts), vocabulary terms, elements of the periodic table, and others.

Based on the suggested ratios of Gickling's model of curriculum-based assessment (Gickling & Havertape, 1981), the procedure attempts to build success and momentum for acquisition of new information. By assessing a student's entry knowledge of the skill to be learned, the evaluator can determine the material the student already knows and the material that they don't. When the new material is taught, the ratio of known to unknown material is maintained at no greater than 70% known and 30% unknown. Thus, a student who is being exposed to new material is never asked to try to learn more than 30% of what is presented. Incremental rehearsal is designed to maximize the number of repetitions to new material within a short period of time, and requires repeated discrimination among items, thereby facilitating the student's progress from the acquisition to the mastery level of learning. Research on the use of incremental rehearsal and its alignment with perspectives on learning and memory is described in Chapter 6 of *Academic Skills Problems, Fifth Edition*. That chapter also describes strategic incremental rehearsal, which is a simplified version using only unknown content, but may result in more efficient learning over time.

The following examples describe the use of incremental rehearsal for use in improving word reading and the acquisition of multiplication facts within a peer-tutoring context. Again, it is important for the reader to recognize that the technique can be applied to any content area where fact-based knowledge needs to be learned.

EXAMPLE: INCREMENTAL REHEARSAL TECHNIQUE
FOR WORD READING AND ORAL READING

The following example describes a process for using incremental rehearsal with oral reading practice to improve reading accuracy. Readers should note that incremental rehearsal does not require the use of an oral reading passage as part of it. There may be situations in which a set of target unknown words has already been identified for a student, in which case Steps 1–3 and 7–9 can be skipped. Otherwise, this example offers a way in which incremental rehearsal can be integrated with text reading practice to improve reading accuracy and efficiency with words in isolation and in text.

- **Step 1.** The evaluator selects a passage for the student to read. The passage should be consistent with content in which the student is currently working on in class. It is important that the passage contain no more than 50% unknown material. This can be assessed by conducting a word search. The evaluator simply asks the student to read various keywords from the passage. If the student misses more than 50% of the words in the word search, the evaluator should select a different passage and repeat the process.

- **Step 2.** The evaluator asks the student to read aloud a portion of the passage (usually a paragraph or two) and times the reading. The evaluator marks the point in the passage reached by the student at the end of 1 minute. The number of words read correctly in this minute is designated as the presession reading fluency.

- **Step 3.** As the student reads, the evaluator notes at least three words with which the student has difficulty reading. On 3″ × 5″ index cards, the evaluator writes the three words (one on each card). These words are designated as *unknowns*. If more than three words can be designated as unknown, the evaluator selects words that are more important for helping the student understand the story.

- **Step 4.** On 3″ × 5″ index cards, the evaluator writes seven words (one on each card) from the passage that the student can read without difficulty. These should be words that are meaningful to the passage, not simply *and, the*, or other nonmeaningful expressions.

- **Step 5.** The session begins with presentation of the first unknown word. If the student has learned skills for decoding unknown words, the evaluator should prompt the student to sound out the word and provide affirmative or corrective feedback. If the student is still developing their decoding skills, the evaluator can model sounding out the word (with pointing to individual letters and letter combinations) and reading it as a whole unit, followed by providing the student with the opportunity to do the same. The evaluator should then define the word for the student and use it in a sentence. Next, the evaluator should ask the student to repeat the definition and use the word in a different sentence.

- **Step 6.** Now the incremental rehearsal begins. After the unknown word is offered, one of the known words is presented. The student is asked to say the word aloud. Next, the unknown word is again presented, followed by the known word previously presented, and then a new known word. This sequence of presentation (unknown followed by known) is continued until all seven knowns and the one unknown word have been presented.

Next, the second unknown word is presented in the same way as the first, with the evaluator and then the student defining it and using it in a sentence. This second unknown word is then folded in among the other seven known words and the first unknown word. In the course of the multiple presentations of the words, the student is asked to sound out the unknown word and repeat its definition whenever they hesitate or are incorrect in the pronunciation of the word. Finally, the third unknown is folded in among the other nine words (two unknown, seven known). Given that the other words were assessed to be known at the starting point, the student should not have difficulty with these words. Figure 10 illustrates the full sequence of presentations for teaching three new words.

• **Step 7.** Upon completion of the incremental rehearsal intervention, the student is asked to reread the passage read in Step 2. The evaluator again marks the number of seconds it took for the student to reach the point in the passage reached at 1 minute during the presession reading. It is important that the student read at least to the same point of the passage that they reached at the beginning of the session; this is necessary to evaluate improvements in their accuracy. The score obtained here is considered the student's postsession reading score.

• **Step 8 (Optional).** Both the pre- and postsession scores can be graphed (by the student, if appropriate). These data can be useful in showing the student the consistent improvement in their reading skills over the short period of time in each session, as well as their improvement in oral reading over days and weeks. However, use caution to prevent the graphing procedure from encouraging speed reading. Emphasize to the student that the goal is to read better and to make reading easier, not necessarily faster.

• **Step 9.** The next session begins by having the student read the next portion of the passage. Following the reading, the 10 words (seven known, three unknown) that were used in the previous session are reviewed. A mark is placed on one of the unknown words to designate that the student knew the word without hesitation during this session.

• **Step 10.** A criterion is set to determine when a previously unknown word is designated as a known word. Typically, this can be defined as getting the word correct on two consecutive sessions after it was introduced.

• **Step 11.** As a new unknown word is added to the drill procedure, one of the original known words is removed from the pile. The first word to be removed is one of the original known words selected at the first session. Each of the other seven known words is replaced with new unknown words. Finally, by the time one of the original unknown words is removed from the pile, it will have been drilled far in excess of the 55 repetitions, thereby providing a basis for the student to reach mastery levels for the new material.

Presentation no.	Unknown item no.	Known item no.	Presentation no.	Unknown item no.	Known item no.	Presentation no.	Unknown item no.	Known item no.
1	1		42		2	83	3	
2		1	43		3	84	2	
3	1		44	2		85	1	
4		1	45	1		86		1
5		2	46		1	87		2
6	1		47		2	88		3
7		1	48		3	89	3	
8		2	49		4	90	2	
9		3	50	2		91	1	
10	1		51	1		92		1
11		1	52		1	93		2
12		2	53		2	94		3
13		3	54		3	95		4
14		4	55		4	96	3	
15	1		56		5	97	2	
16		1	57	2		98	1	
17		2	58	1		99		1
18		3	59		1	100		2
19		4	60		2	101		3
20		5	61		3	102		4
21	1		62		4	103		5
22		1	63		5	104	3	
23		2	64		6	105	2	
24		3	65	2		106	1	
25		4	66	1		107		1
26		5	67		1	108		2
27		6	68		2	109		3
28	1		69		3	110		4
29		1	70		4	111		5
30		2	71		5	112		6
31		3	72		6	113	3	
32		4	73		7	114	2	
33		5	74	3		115	1	
34		6	75	2		116		1
35		7	76	1		117		2
36	2		77		1	118		3
37	1		78	3		119		4
38		1	79	2		120		5
39	2		80	1		121		6
40	1		81		1	122		7
41		1	82		2			

FIGURE 10. Sequences for presenting known and unknown materials in the incremental rehearsal technique, assuming 10 items (3 unknown and 7 known).

EXAMPLE: INCREMENTAL REHEARSAL TECHNIQUE FOR MULTIPLICATION NUMBER COMBINATIONS

In the following example, incremental rehearsal is used to teach multiplication number combinations (i.e., math facts). The same process is used for teaching addition, subtraction, and division number combinations. As described in Chapter 6 of *Academic Skills Problems, Fifth Edition*, before using this drill, students learn a fallback strategy for determining the answer to an unknown number combination using a counting strategy or a number line. Students should be encouraged to memorize number combinations through instruction and practice, but when memory fails, they should be prompted to use their strategies to identify the correct answer. Additionally, students can learn number combinations more efficiently by targeting number combinations systematically (i.e., learning fact families together and in a logical sequence), as described in Chapter 6 of *Academic Skills Problems, Fifth Edition*. The following example is presented in a peer-tutoring context; however, it can easily be adapted to be implemented by an adult interventionist.

Students: Two boys in third grade have been referred for problems in learning multiplication number combinations.

Preassessment Phase: To determine the number of known and unknown facts, the students are administered a quiz in which they are asked to answer all computational problems with fact families 1–9. The number of problems not completed or incorrect provides an indication of the facts that the students have and have not learned.

Instructional Structure: The procedure is set up as a peer-tutoring activity. The students are taught the procedure and are required to conduct 10-minute tutoring sessions in which they drill each other using the incremental rehearsal technique. This strategy requires multiplication fact flashcards with the answer on the reverse side.

- **Step 1.** Each student selects seven cards from their pile of pre-assessed known facts.

- **Step 2.** Each student selects one card from their pile of unknown pre-assessed facts.

- **Step 3.** The teacher informs the two students that they have 20 minutes for tutoring.

- **Step 4.** The students decide who will first serve as the "teacher" (roles will switch later in the session). After it is decided which student will begin the tutoring, the incremental rehearsal procedure commences. The teacher of the pair presents the first unknown fact to the learner. The teacher models the fact, for example, "five times three is fifteen." The learner repeats. The learner can also be prompted to use a counting strategy or number line to determine the answer, but before proceeding, the learner should say the full number combination sentence out loud for the unknown fact (e.g., "five times three is fifteen").

• **Step 5.** The teacher then presents a known fact, followed by the unknown fact, the first known fact, and another known fact. The unknown fact is presented sequentially in this fashion until all seven known facts have been presented and folded in among the unknown facts. (See Figure 10 for the presentation sequence.) The learner need only say the answer for each problem (i.e., the full sentence is used for introducing new facts or error correction).

• **Step 6.** The eight facts (one unknown and seven known) are shuffled. The second unknown fact is then presented and folded in among the other eight facts. This is repeated again for the third unknown fact.

• **Step 7.** If the student hesitates or is incorrect on any fact, the teacher instructs them to complete a brief correction procedure. The teacher prompts the student the correct answer using a counting strategy or number line and then says the number combination sentence aloud. The incorrect fact is then presented again to the learner.

• **Step 8.** When all facts have been folded in, the entire group of 10 facts is presented three times. Each time, the packet of index cards is shuffled to prevent the learner from simply remembering the sequence of responses.

• **Step 9.** The final step is a test of the 10 facts that the students have practiced. On this test, a mark is placed on the unknown fact cards if a student is correct on this trial. When an unknown fact attains three consecutive marks, it is now considered to be a learned fact.

• **Step 10.** The number of new facts learned each week is graphed by the students. In addition, the teacher administers weekly curriculum-based measurement math probes taken from across all fact families. These data are also graphed to evaluate progress.

Cover–Copy–Compare

The *cover–copy–compare* (CCC) technique has been found to be useful for students who need practice and drill in moving skills from the stage of acquisition to mastery. First described by Skinner and his colleagues for use in mastering multiplication facts in elementary students (Skinner, Turco, et al., 1989), the technique has been applied to skill areas such as the learning of geography facts (Skinner, Belifore, et al., 1992), science knowledge (Smith et al., 2002), and spelling (Erion et al., 2009). A benefit of CCC is that it offers a way to allow students to practice content independently while ensuring they receive feedback on the accuracy of their responses. Chapter 6 of *Academic Skills Problems, Fifth Edition* reviews other research on the use of CCC across academic skills.

Despite changes in content, the basic technique is the same. Based on the technique as originally described by Skinner et al. (1989) for teaching basic multiplication number combinations in elementary-age students, the student first studies a problem, covers the problem with an index card, writes the problem and solution in the next column, uncovers the problem and solution, and evaluates their response. The systematic nature of the practice offers an easily structured approach for students who need to rehearse and learn fact-based information, and it can be used in almost any content area. In the area of mathematics facts, CCC worksheets can be easily generated by a computer program available from *interventioncentral.org*.

Two examples of the CCC technique are provided here. Figure 11 is an example of a form useful for implementing CCC in mathematics; in this case, for addition facts with sums to 18. Figure 12 is an adaptation of the CCC technique for spelling, in which the student studies the word, covers the word, writes the word, and then evaluates their response. If incorrect, the student is instructed to write the word three times in the area provided.

Addition: Two one-digit numbers: Sums to 18.

Student: _____   Date: _____

Item 1: 2 CD/2 CD Total $\begin{array}{r} 8 \\ +\,9 \\ \hline \mathbf{17} \end{array}$	$\begin{array}{r} 8 \\ +\,9 \\ \hline \end{array}$ CORRECT?
Item 2: 2 CD/2 CD Total $\begin{array}{r} 7 \\ +\,1 \\ \hline \mathbf{8} \end{array}$	$\begin{array}{r} 7 \\ +\,1 \\ \hline \end{array}$ CORRECT?
Item 3: 2 CD/2 CD Total $\begin{array}{r} 6 \\ +\,1 \\ \hline \mathbf{7} \end{array}$	$\begin{array}{r} 6 \\ +\,1 \\ \hline \end{array}$ CORRECT?
Item 4: 2 CD/2 CD Total $\begin{array}{r} 4 \\ +\,4 \\ \hline \mathbf{8} \end{array}$	$\begin{array}{r} 4 \\ +\,4 \\ \hline \end{array}$ CORRECT?
Item 5: 2 CD/2 CD Total $\begin{array}{r} 6 \\ +\,1 \\ \hline \mathbf{7} \end{array}$	$\begin{array}{r} 6 \\ +\,1 \\ \hline \end{array}$ CORRECT?
Item 6: 2 CD/2 CD Total $\begin{array}{r} 4 \\ +\,1 \\ \hline \mathbf{5} \end{array}$	$\begin{array}{r} 4 \\ +\,1 \\ \hline \end{array}$ CORRECT?
Item 7: 2 CD/2 CD Total $\begin{array}{r} 7 \\ +\,8 \\ \hline \mathbf{15} \end{array}$	$\begin{array}{r} 7 \\ +\,8 \\ \hline \end{array}$ CORRECT?
Item 8: 2 CD/2 CD Total $\begin{array}{r} 2 \\ +\,6 \\ \hline \mathbf{8} \end{array}$	$\begin{array}{r} 2 \\ +\,6 \\ \hline \end{array}$ CORRECT?
Item 9: 2 CD/2 CD Total $\begin{array}{r} 5 \\ +\,4 \\ \hline \mathbf{9} \end{array}$	$\begin{array}{r} 5 \\ +\,4 \\ \hline \end{array}$ CORRECT?

FIGURE 11. Example of a CCC worksheet for addition facts to 18. CD, correct digits.

Study the word	Cover the word and write it	Compare— Did I get it?		If not, try again
1.		yes	no	
2.		yes	no	
3.		yes	no	
4.		yes	no	
5.		yes	no	
6.		yes	no	
7.		yes	no	
8.		yes	no	
9.		yes	no	
10.		yes	no	

FIGURE 12. Example of a CCC worksheet for spelling.

EXAMPLE: CCC FOR ADDITION FACTS, SUMS TO 18

- **Step 1.** Student examines the problem.
- **Step 2.** Student covers the problem with index card.
- **Step 3.** Student writes the problem and solution on the right side of the paper.
- **Step 4.** Student uncovers the problem and solution.
- **Step 5.** Student evaluates whether their written response matches the model.

EXAMPLE: CCC FOR SPELLING

- **Step 1.** Student studies the word and spells it to themself.
- **Step 2.** Student covers the word with index card.

- **Step 3.** Student writes the word on the right side of the paper.

- **Step 4.** Student uncovers the word.

- **Step 5.** Student evaluates whether their written response matches the model.

- **Step 6.** If their response is correct, the student moves to the next word; if their response is incorrect, they writes the correct spelling three times.

Progress Monitoring

Graphing and Interpreting Data

A key component of progress monitoring involves depicting the data in graphed form. Such graphic displays serve to improve the evaluator's understanding of the data because graphs help make trends and changes in scores that are more apparent compared to viewing only a series of numbers. Progress monitoring graphs also offer ways to communicate data with parents, teachers, and students themselves about student progress. Indeed, the process of collecting and reporting the data in graphed form can itself serve as a strong motivator and reinforcement for some students.

Provided below are instructions for setting up hand-drawn graphs. However, technological advances suggest that evaluators should use existing graphing tools to display and manage the data. All major vendors of CBM tools (Acadience, AIMSweb, DIBELS, easyCBM, FastBridge) offer resources for entering and graphing progress monitoring data. Spreadsheet programs such as Microsoft Excel and Google Sheets are common tools that can easily be used for graphing purposes. Resources for using Microsoft Excel for progress monitoring graphs may be found on the Intervention Central website (*www.interventioncentral.org*). We maintain the instructions for creating graphs by hand for two reasons: (1) From a learning standpoint, they provide a new evaluator with a better sense of what goes into the graph and how it is set up. A better sense of what is "under the hood" helps in evaluating graphing programs offered by CBM vendors, and also makes transitioning to a software graph easier. (2) It provides skills that could be helpful if software resources are not available.

SETTING UP GRAPHIC DISPLAYS

Graphic displays of data are useful for both short- and long-term monitoring. The setting-up process is similar for all types of graphs.

• **Step 1.** Identify the metric that is being used for data collection purposes. This can be words read correctly or per minute, number of mathematics problems completed per minute, cumulative problems learned, number of words spelled correctly, number of correct writing sequences, or other such measures.

• **Step 2.** Identify the possible range that the metric used for data collection can occupy. This is usually the set of numbers representing the lower and upper limits in which scores may occur.

• **Step 3.** The metric used for data collection becomes the range placed on the y (vertical) axis. Divide the range into equal units and write these along the vertical axis.

• **Step 4.** Identify the amount of time across which the data will be collected. This can be any unit of time up to a full school year.

• **Step 5.** The amount of time for data collection becomes the range placed on the x (horizontal) axis. Divide the range into equal units (sessions, days, weeks, months, etc.).

The data are plotted by placing points on the graph. Each data point is the student's score on the progress monitoring measure for each time the data are collected.

Graphs are usually divided by the particular phase of the intervention. Data obtained during baseline (i.e., before an intervention begins) and intervention phases are separated by a solid line drawn on the graph. The data are also not connected by lines across these two phases. Once the intervention begins, changes in the intervention procedure are designated by broken lines, with the data again not being connected through those phases.

Figure 13 shows a progress monitoring graph for a first-grade student for whom two interventions—peer tutoring and peer tutoring plus cover–copy–compare—were implemented to improve their performance on the acquisition of basic math facts in addition and subtraction. The intervention took place over 15 weeks (one semester). Baseline and intervention phases are separated by a solid line, and the two intervention phases are separated by a broken line.

PREPARING CBM-TYPE GRAPHS

The purpose of collecting progress monitoring data is to inform instructional decisions, such as determining when an intervention is effective and should continue, versus recognizing when an intervention should be adjusted to improve a student's progress. Making these types of decisions is made possible by setting up a progress monitoring graph that includes the student's goal, which refers to a target score the student is expected to attain before the end of the progress monitoring period. Setting a goal allows the user to connect the student's initial score (i.e., baseline) with the goal, thereby creating an aimline that reflects an ideal rate of growth needed to achieve the goal. Methods for setting progress monitoring goals, and the pros and

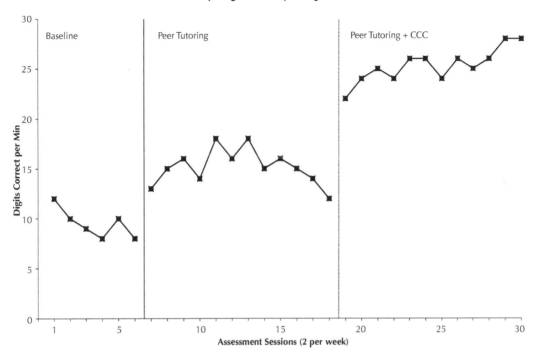

FIGURE 13. Example of mathematics progress monitoring data for a first-grade student for whom peer tutoring and peer tutoring plus CCC were used as interventions.

cons of each, are detailed in Chapter 7 of *Academic Skills Problems, Fifth Edition.* The following is an example of one of these methods, which uses a percentile level of achievement based on normative data for setting a goal in CBM oral reading. The same process would be used if the target skill involves mathematics, spelling, or writing.

Dan is a beginning third-grade student. Baseline data taken over 3 days show that Dan is reading at 48 words correct per minute (WCPM), 30 WCPM, and 53 WCPM in third-grade material. Using scores collected during a local norming project of Dan's school district, the teacher elects to set a yearly goal for Dan to read at the 50th percentile of third-grade readers by the end of the year—that is, a goal of 90 WCPM. Note that the 50th percentile was chosen as a goal for Dan based on his baseline scores; the 50th percentile may not necessarily represent an ideal goal for other students, especially students with lower baseline skills.

Figure 14 shows the CBM graph generated for Dan. In the figure, Dan's baseline is represented by the median score across the three baseline data sessions (48 WCPM). A goal of 90 WCPM at the end of a 36-week period (1 academic year from the time the data collection is started in September) is indicated on the graph, and a solid line connecting the baseline and goal is drawn. This line represents Dan's aimline. As data are collected over time, it is anticipated that Dan's performance will match this line of progress. If his scores consistently exceed the aimline, then the teacher may decide to increase the goal originally set for Dan. If his scores are consistently below the aimline or move in a direction opposite to that shown by the aimline, the teacher should decide to alter the instructional technique to improve

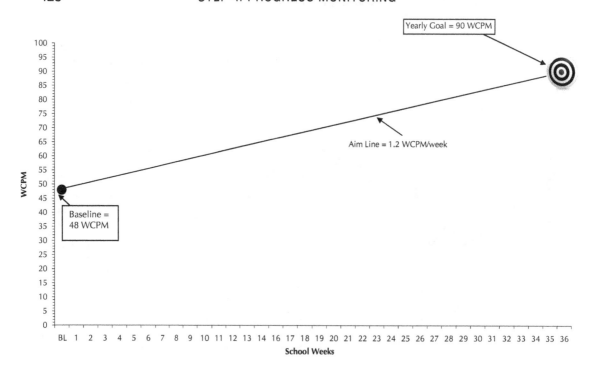

FIGURE 14. CBM graph showing Dan's baseline performance and expected rate of progress in reading across a school year.

Dan's performance. Also with the goal of 90 WCPM, Dan is expected to improve his oral reading fluency by 1.2 WCPM each week; this is his slope of targeted rate of improvement (90 WCPM – 48 WCPM = 42 WCPM ÷ 36 weeks = 1.2 WCPM/week).

INTERPRETING GRAPHED CBM DATA
AND MAKING INSTRUCTIONAL DECISIONS

Progress monitoring data in all academic areas are evaluated to determine whether the student is improving their skills at an expected rate, which indicates that an intervention is having its intended effect, or if adjustments to the intervention should be made to improve the student's rate of progress. Progress monitoring data can also be evaluated to determine if the student has met their goal, in which case the intensity of the intervention might be reduced or the goal might be increased. Examining a student's progress monitoring data to make these types of decisions requires methods for evaluating the student's trend and a set of rules for determining an appropriate instructional decision.

In Chapter 7 of *Academic Skills Problems, Fifth Edition,* we described two primary methods for evaluating a student's trend relative to their expected rate of growth (i.e., aimline). *Point rules* involve examining the most recent three data points and determining whether they are above or below the aimline. When some (or all) of the data points fall above the aimline, it is an indication that the student is progressing at the expected rate and that the intervention is having its intended effect. In contrast, when all three of the most recent data points fall below the aimline, it can be viewed as an indication that the student's progress is below expectations. In these cases, adjustments or changes to the intervention or aspects of its implementation (e.g., frequency, duration, location, makeup of the group) might be considered. The second method for evaluating a student's trend are *slope rules*. Slope rules require an ordinary least squares (OLS) trendline (i.e., slope) fitted to the student's data, which can be easily added when using a spreadsheet program like Excel or Google Sheets. Additionally, most CBM providers offer options for graphing students' progress monitoring data and often automatically add the student's OLS trendline. Slope rules involve examining the student's trendline relative to the aimline and the goal. A trendline that is as steep or steeper than the aimline, and suggests the student is on a trajectory to accomplish the goal, indicates the intervention is having its desired effect. On the other hand, a trendline that is less steep and reflects a trajectory in which the student will not meet their goal indicates a need to consider adjustments to the intervention.

In Chapter 7 of *Academic Skills Problems, Fifth Edition*, we discussed pros and cons of point rules and slope rules. However, nothing prevents one from considering both in informing their instructional decisions. Requirements of using these methods to make decisions are that (1) sufficient time has elapsed to expect some growth in the target skill, and (2) a sufficient number of data points have been collected to have confidence that the student's trend is relatively stable. If there appear to be too few data points (e.g., some recommend having at least 6 data points), or if the data are highly variable, it may be best to collect a few more data points to see if the trendline stabilizes.

An additional set of decisions pertains to knowing when to raise a progress monitoring goal or consider reducing the intensity of an intervention (or removing it if no longer needed). As discussed in Chapter 7 of *Academic Skills Problems, Fifth Edition*, raising a goal should only be considered if the student has actually achieved the goal on more than one occasion, or if it becomes apparent that the initial goal was set in error or not ambitious enough.

Exercise 13 provides an opportunity to practice making decisions based on a series of progress monitoring graphs.

Making Instructional Decisions
Based on Progress Monitoring Graphs

This exercise provides practice in applying decision rules to progress monitoring data. Progress monitoring graphs are a primary mechanism for implementing responsive, data-driven interventions. Therefore, developing skills to effectively "read" progress monitoring graphs is an important part of ongoing support for students with academic difficulties.

Your task in this exercise is to make decisions for a series of progress monitoring graphs and indicate your rationale for each decision. The student's goal in all graphs (75 points) is indicated by the square on the right side of each graph, and the solid line connecting the student's baseline score to the goal is the aimline. The dashed line is the student's trendline based on the data points entered so far. Although you do not have access to other information about the student and the intervention that is important to consider when making decisions, this activity will nevertheless provide practice in evaluating progress monitoring data using a set of decision rules. For each graph, indicate one of the following decisions and the reasons for your decision:

A. More data are needed to make a decision.
B. Continue the current intervention.
C. Consider adjusting the intervention.
D. Raise the goal or consider reducing the intensity of the intervention.

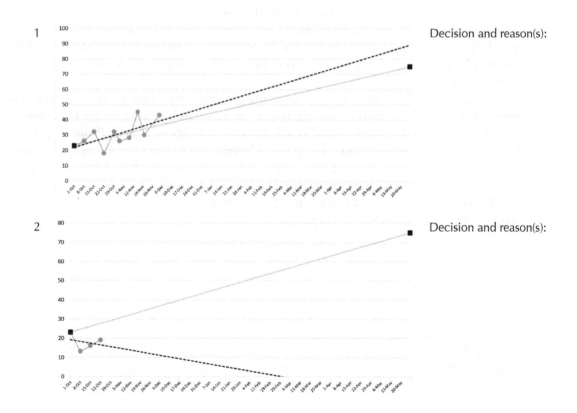

1   Decision and reason(s):

2   Decision and reason(s):

130

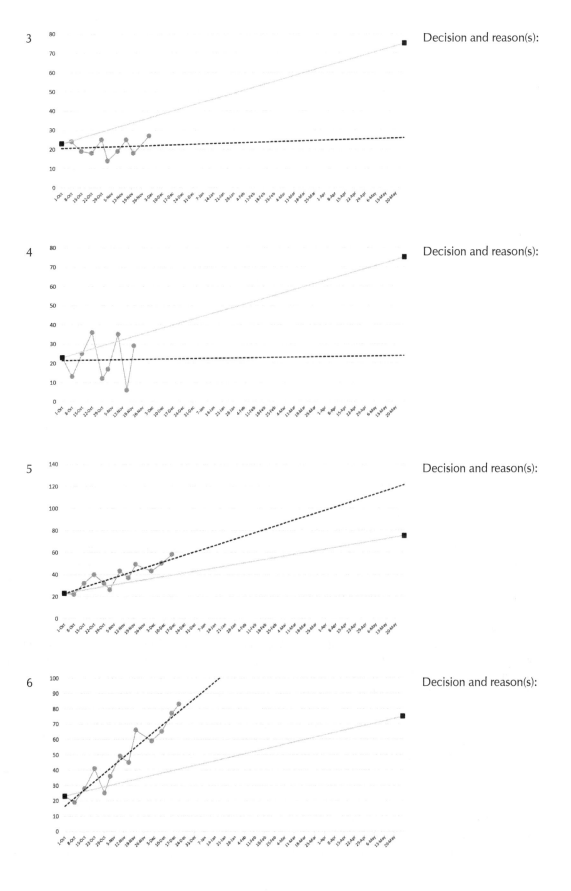

3   Decision and reason(s):

4   Decision and reason(s):

5   Decision and reason(s):

6   Decision and reason(s):

131

Answers for Exercise 13

Graph 1. The best answer for the first graph is *continue the current intervention*. Two of the most recent three data points are above the aimline, and the student's trendline is steeper than the aimline. Thus, both the point and slope rules indicate that the student is making progress consistent with the targeted rate of growth and the intervention is successful so far. Because the student's trendline places them on a trajectory to exceed their goal of 75 points by the end of the year, readers might be tempted to suggest raising the goal. However, this may not be a wise decision at this time because the student's most recent scores are still well below that level. Students sometimes show rapid growth in the initial stages of an intervention, after which their rate of growth can level off. It would be best to let the current intervention continue with the current goal and re-evaluate at subsequent decision points.

Graph 2. *More data are needed* is probably the best decision for the second graph. Excluding the baseline score, only three data points have been collected. Although it may appear alarming that the student's trendline indicates a decline in progress, the intervention has only been implemented for a few weeks. Other information about the student or the intervention implementation would certainly aid any decisions at this point, but the limited amount of data and duration of the intervention does not permit much confidence in the stability of the student's trend. It may be best to collect a few more data points and re-evaluate.

Graph 3. If you said *consider adjusting the intervention*, you made a good decision. The student's most recent three data points fall below the aimline, and the student's trendline is nearly flat and well below the aimline. This would be an important time to consider the intervention that is being implemented and what adjustments could be made. As discussed in Chapter 7 of *Academic Skills Problems, Fifth Edition*, a range of adjustments could be considered and should be influenced by other information about the student and the intervention, including the use of brief diagnostic assessments or permanent product reviews, as needed. Adjustments could involve adding components or strategies to the existing program or changing the program itself. However, drastic changes should not be made if less invasive adjustments may be equally (or more) beneficial. It may be that adjustments to how the intervention is implemented may be appropriate, such as increasing the amount of practice or response opportunities the student is provided, increasing the dosage (i.e., increasing frequency per week or duration of each session), improving fidelity of implementation, changing the group size or the students in the group, slowing the pace in which new content is introduced, embedding more frequent and systematic review, or reteaching skills or concepts that the student had not mastered or retained.

Graph 4. For the fourth graph, *more data are needed* is probably the best decision. Although eight data points have been collected, the student's scores are highly variable, which affects the stability of the trendline. One of the three most recent data points is above the aimline; however, the overall trendline is flat. It may be best to collect a couple more data points but not wait too long to make an instructional adjustment if their overall trend remains below the aimline. Other data and information about the student's achievement should also be considered, which could reveal that a better decision might be to *adjust the current intervention*. The data in Graph 4 also indicate a need to consider why scores are so variable. It may be that the difficulty of each probe varies too much (i.e., probes are not equivalent enough), in which case a different set of probes that is better controlled for difficulty might be considered. Or, the evaluator might consider the student's mood and level of engagement in the progress monitoring sessions; it may be that the extremely low scores occurred on days in which the student was more distractable or less motivated. Finally, the evaluator should examine the fidelity with which the progress monitoring measures are being collected and ensure that probes are being administered following the standardized procedures every time (e.g., correct time limits are being used consistently, responses are scored the same way). Inconsistency in how the probes are administered or scored will result in wide fluctuations in scores and will usually render the data unusable. Overall, the pattern of scores depicted in the fourth graph, with a lot of variability and some ambiguity on what to decide, can be common for students with academic difficulties.

Graph 5. If you responded to the fifth graph with *continue the current intervention,* good work! The student is clearly responding well to the intervention, as indicated by both the point and slope rules. Similar to the first graph, it may be tempting to suggest raising the student's goal. However, the student has not yet achieved scores that meet or exceed their goal of 75. In this case, letting the current intervention continue and re-evaluating the data in the near future is probably the best choice.

Graph 6. *Raise the goal or consider reducing the intensity of the intervention* is a good response to the sixth graph. The student has made rapid progress, and their most recent scores of 77 and 83 both exceed their goal score of 75. This may be a time to consider raising the goal if it was originally set to be less ambitious or represented a lower level of achievement (e.g., meeting the 25th percentile). On the other hand, if the goal was ambitious and represented a typical level of achievement for a student in this grade level (e.g., above the 40th percentile), it may be that the intervention is no longer needed at its current intensity and the frequency or duration might be reduced. It may also be that the student's skill difficulties have been remediated and supplemental intervention is not needed anymore. This decision should be considered carefully and in conjunction with other data and information about the student's achievement and classroom functioning. Even if the intervention is reduced or eliminated, continuing to monitor progress for a period of time can indicate whether the student maintains the gains they made.

Developing Local Norms

Given that many schools and school districts are conducting universal screening as part of efforts to establish early intervention and the implementation of multi-tiered systems of support (MTSS) and response-to-intervention (RTI) models, local norms are often already available from these data. Many assessment systems that schools use include resources for automatically generating local normative data. However, in districts wishing to develop local norms where such systems or screening models are not present, or if schools wish to collect local norms in skill areas not covered by their current assessment systems (e.g., mathematics or writing), well-developed methods for doing so are available. Shinn (1988, 1989) provides a discussion of this process and offers step-by-step directions on how to construct these norms. Specifically, Shinn (1988) notes that one must (1) create a measurement net that defines the appropriate skills and materials for assessment, (2) establish a normative sampling plan, (3) train data collectors, (4) collect the data, and (5) summarize the data. Gathering data that represent the performance of students within the schools where the data will be used provides a strong sense of ownership of the outcomes, and increases the certainty that the data comparison will be representative of the community.

To illustrate this process, the steps involved in the collection of local norms in reading for elementary school students from a medium-size urban school district are described. Readers should note that the sampling procedures used here are different from those recommended by Shinn (1988). The normative data from three districts are also presented, each representing high, moderate, and low levels of socioeconomic status, as defined by the percentage of low-income families in the district. Readers should note that, although reading is the skill of interest in the following example, the procedure is the same if normative data are collected in other academic skill areas, such as spelling, mathematics, or writing.

CREATING THE MEASUREMENT NET

Schools typically use published reading passages for purposes of norming or universal screening. These passages have been carefully calibrated for grade-level readability. Such passages are commercially available in products such as Acdience, AIMSweb®, DIBELS, and easyCBM, among others. The advantage of using these passages is that students have not typically encountered them, thus avoiding any practice effects from repeated reading. In addition, the passages are generally well controlled for readability so that difficulty level across passages is less likely to result in differences in student performance within grade levels.

Although many school districts develop norms using these generic reading passages, the particular school district presented as an example at the time of the norm development wanted to use its own reading series to conduct the norms. Data were collected three times during the year: fall (October), winter (February), and spring (May). The reading levels of average students within grades were inconsistent across the district. At some schools, students were reading at levels commensurate with the publisher's assessment of grade level of the material; in other schools, the majority of students were reading approximately one level (or book) behind. When this discrepancy was discussed, the school district decided to use the publisher-recommended grade-level material as the measures to be assessed. Passages for assessment were taken from materials that constituted the end-of-year goals for students in each grade, and each passage selected was evaluated using the Spache readability formula. Only passages that had readability levels within the grade-level book from which the passage was taken were used (see Table 1).

Randomly selected passages of between 150 and 200 words were selected from each book, according to standard CBM procedures. Passages were retyped on separate pages for presentation.

SELECTING THE SAMPLE

When districts are conducting universal screening, the selection of the sample is not of concern since the entire school population is being assessed. However, when local norms are being collected and not all schools are involved in the data collection process, issues of sample selection become very important. Given the size of the

TABLE 1. Measurement Net in Reading for Norming

Grade	Name of book	Publisher's assigned grade level
1	*Surprise*	1.4[a]
2	*Friends*	2.1[b]
3	*Just Listen*	3.1[b]
4	*Dinosauring*	4
5	*Explore*	5

[a]Indicates fourth book of grade level.
[b]Indicates first book of grade level.

school district and resources available for data collection in the example presented here, it was not possible simply to select students randomly from across the district, as is often recommended in the process of obtaining local norms. In addition, the school district included a wide range of socioeconomic and academic ability levels that needed to be equally represented in the sample.

To address the problems of the resources available to collect the data, it was decided to concentrate the normative sample on six elementary schools. In considering the wide range of socioeconomic levels, the school district administrators identified six schools, two each that represented lower (L), lower-middle (LM), and middle (M) socioeconomic levels (with the three levels characterizing the district). To validate the selection of these schools, the percentages of students eliogible for free or reduced-price meals in the three schools were compared. At the identified L schools, 93% of the students were eligible for free or reduced-price meals; at the LM schools, 56%; and at the M schools, 23%. Thus, these schools appeared to accurately represent the range of socioeconomic levels in the district.

The next step was to develop a sample that would fairly represent the range of reading abilities within each of these schools. To accomplish this, prior to each scheduled assessment, the reading specialist assigned to each school provided a list of the current placement within the reading series of all students in that building. These data were used to identify the proportion of students in each grade within a building at each level of the reading series. For example, in the L schools, it was found that in the third grade, 10% of the students were reading *Dinosauring* (a fourth-grade book), 30% were reading *Just Listen* (the first book in third grade), 50% were reading *Friends* (the first book in second grade), 8% were reading *Surprises* (the fourth book in the first grade), and 2% were reading below the first-grade level.

A normative sample consisting of 900 students was developed, representing approximately 25% of the population in the three schools. From each school, 150 students (30 per grade) were selected. The normative sample within each school was constructed by selecting an identical proportion of students from each level of the reading series within each grade within each school. For example, to select the students from the third grade in the L school, the list of students assigned the *Just Listen* book was obtained. As noted earlier, this represented 30% of the third-grade students. Given that the final sample from the third grade of the L schools would have 30 students, a total of 4 (15% of 30) would be selected at random from among the possible 15% for inclusion in the normative sample. This process was repeated for each grade level and each school, in order to end up with a final sample whose representation was proportional to the percentage of students at the various reading levels of the grade.

DATA COLLECTION

Data were collected over 2-week periods in October, February, and May during the school year. Graduate students in school psychology and special education served as data collectors. Students were tested on an individual basis in a small room adjacent to the classrooms in each of the school buildings. Each student was asked to read a passage aloud and was timed for 1 minute. The number of words read correctly per minute was calculated according to standard CBM techniques. Errors included mispronunciations, omissions, and substitutions.

DATA ANALYSIS AND RESULTS

Results obtained from the normative data collection can be displayed in numerous ways. Table 2 and Figure 15 show the overall outcomes for the entire district. Such data as these can be used as benchmarks for a district's expectations and performance.

An important concern in using local norms is recognizing that the overall level of academic performance across school districts is likely to vary considerably. One of the factors correlated with overall student achievement is the overall socioeconomic status (SES) of the community in the district. Table 3 provides data from three districts where local norms were collected. One of the districts has a high number of families experiencing lower income (59.5%), the second a moderate level of low-income families (32.8%), and the third a small number of low-income families (6.3%). As can be seen in Table 3, reading performance varied greatly across these districts. For example, students assessed in the spring of the third grade, who scored at the 25th percentile, ranged from 44 WCPM in the low-SES district, 89 WCPM in the moderate-SES district, and 102 WCPM in the high-SES district. Although the differences lessened as students reached the fifth-grade level, there was still a difference of 33 WCPM between the low- and high-SES districts. Clearly, using local norms allows for consideration of students' performance within their context and

TABLE 2. Quartiles for Local Norms in Reading from Grade-Level Reading Material for a Medium-Size Urban District in the Northeastern United States

Grade	Percentile	Fall	Winter	Spring
1	25th	1	2	6
	50th	2	5	13
	75th	6	15	35
2	25th	11	21	31
	50th	26	38	53
	75th	38	74	85
3	25th	36	38	44
	50th	50	63	78
	75th	81	95	118
4	25th	53	59	75
	50th	73	81	92
	75th	98	110	120
5	25th	77	83	88
	50th	98	110	121
	75th	130	142	151

Fall

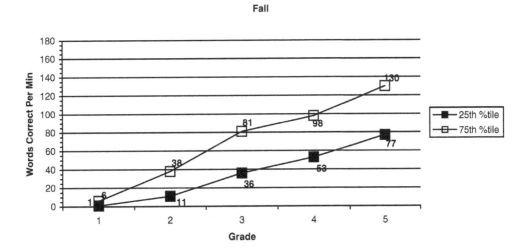

Winter

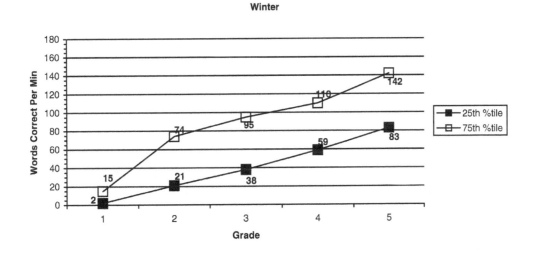

Spring

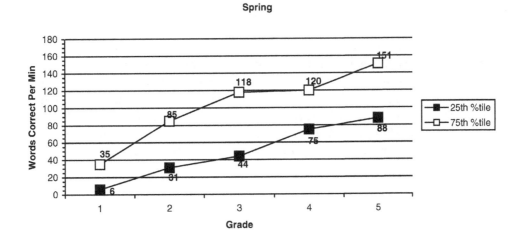

FIGURE 15. Normative data in reading from midsize urban school district showing 25th and 75th percentiles across grades and assessment periods.

TABLE 3. Words Correct per Minute Scores at the 25th Percentile across Three School Districts from High, Moderate, and Low Socioeconomic Bases

	Fall	Winter	Spring
Grade 1			
High	4	29	59
Moderate	4	15	26
Low	1	2	6
Grade 2			
High	31	69	79
Moderate	31	55	67
Low	11	21	31
Grade 3			
High	68	86	102
Moderate	62	77	89
Low	36	38	44
Grade 4			
High	80	98	114
Moderate	83	96	104
Low	53	59	75
Grade 5			
High	103	113	121
Moderate	90	101	115
Low	77	83	88

community and provides a basis for considering the sources of opportunity, disadvantage, and marginalization that children experience. Using data such as those in Table 3 can allow a district to consider their context in setting ambitious goals.

Although the example presented here used reading material that was from the district's curriculum of instruction, it is neither required nor recommended that districts develop their own passages for norming purposes. Standard reading passages that are closely controlled for grade-based readability are available from both commercial and free sites. Readers may want to examine these sources for reading passages that have been found to be effective in conducting local norms in reading. Such passages are available commercially from several sources, such as Acadience, AIMSweb, DIBELS, easyCBM, and Fastbridge, among others. Materials for assessing prereading skills, as well as skills in mathematics and writing, are also available from some of these sources. Also, Hasbrouck and Tindal (2017) have compiled a set of norms from multiple norming projects that can provide reasonable estimates of normative performance for students nationwide. These norms are provided in Chapter 7 of *Academic Skills Problems, Fifth Edition,* and are also publicly available at *www.brtprojects.org/wp-content/uploads/2017/10/TechRpt_1702ORFNorms_Fini.pdf.*

Tools for Multi-Tiered Systems of Support: Data-Based Decision Making

The 2004 reauthorization of the Individuals with Disabilities Education Act (IDEA) introduced response to intervention (RTI) as an alternative method to the well-known process of determining the discrepancy between a student's ability and their achievement as the basis for the identification of particular learning disabilities. Specifically, IDEA allows that a process which determines if students respond to scientific, research-based intervention can be used as an alternative to the well-known ability–achievement discrepancy. When using RTI for determining a specific learning disability (SLD), one needs to show substantial differences between the referred student and similar-age/grade peers in both level of performance and the rate at which they improve when provided with instructional interventions known to be highly effective when implemented with strong integrity.

Over the years, perhaps more importantly than its methodology for determining the presence of an SLD, RTI became viewed as a system of prevention and early intervention focused on improving student academic skills or behavior. To differentiate the school–system framework of prevention and intervention from the RTI process of disability identification, the field adopted the term *multi-tiered systems of support* (MTSS). The processes that are considered to be key components of MTSS form a framework for schoolwide implementation of effective instruction and support for all students. Having high-quality core instruction and a system of intervention support makes it possible to use RTI as a means of identifying students with an SLD. Likewise, schools that choose not to use the RTI model for purposes of identifying SLD can still implement an MTSS model as a means of delivering effective instructional services to all children in both general and special education (Fuchs, 2003; National Association of State Directors of Special Education, 2006; Vaughn et al., 2007).

Most models of MTSS consist of a common set of characteristics that include high-quality core instruction and a multi-tiered approach to intervention (Marston et al., 2003); universal screening of all students (Fuchs, 2003; Gresham, 2002); small-group and multi-tiered instruction delivered to students according to their skill needs (Brown-Chidsey & Steege, 2010; Brown-Chidsey et al., 2009; Vaughn et al., 2003); team structures to manage and analyze data collected through the process; and progress monitoring of student performance to assess the impact of interventions (Marston et al., 2003; Shapiro et al., 2010). Among these components, the effective collection, use, and interpretation of data related to student performance lie at the heart of the model.

Models of MTSS vary somewhat by the context in which they are implemented. In some high-performing schools, implementers of the model need to consider how to effectively accommodate the large number of general education students who are highly proficient, allowing these students to reach levels beyond the expectations of typical grade-level performers. Likewise, in low-performing schools, implementers need to consider how to address the large numbers of general education students who are functioning below grade-level expectations, while also providing effective interventions for those students who are at serious risk for persistent academic difficulties. Regardless of the context of the model, however, all MTSS models are driven by data-based decision-making. Educators' opinions and perceptions, although still important, must be supported by data as the underlying basis of the perspective. The school culture is driven by improving student outcomes, which are shown via data collection on student performance.

To effectively implement a data-based decision-making process, schools need tools. Each school will find the data tools that work best in that particular context. Here, we provide a variety of tools found to be useful in clinical practice across multiple MTSS implementations. Each tool is presented consistent with the components of the data-based decision-making process. Specifically, tools are provided to evaluate the fidelity of implementation of data-based decision-making meetings, to assist in the setting of grade-based group goals for student performance, and to assist in making data-based individual decisions. Although some of the tools presented here were developed for MTSS implementation in reading within the elementary school level, but can easily be adapted for other academic skills and grade ranges. Additional tools relevant to MTSS implementation across academic skill areas may be found in Shapiro et al. (2011).

LEVELS OF IMPLEMENTATION—DATA ANALYSIS

The data analysis process within MTSS models is facilitated by school teams. Typically, two levels of teams are present in MTSS implementations, although some schools may combine these two teams into a single unit. The *core team* includes on-site key professionals with skills and passion for data analysis and could potentially include anyone working in that school (school psychologists, counselors, general education teachers, special education teachers, intervention specialists). Core teams usually have responsibilities that cut across grades and are headed by the school's senior leadership, such as the principal or assistant principal. The core team often makes initial recommendations for student assignment to intervention groups based on its analysis of the data. The core team also usually sets the grade-level goals related to student outcomes and considers the strategies that are needed at the level of the core program (Tier 1) to ensure overall student success. Considerations of the implementation fidelity of overall instruction as well as the effectiveness of identified interventions at Tiers 2 and 3 are a part of the team's responsibilities.

The *grade-level* team usually consists of all teaching staff at a specific grade level. Included would be those providing support in programs such as Title I (i.e., federally funded remedial programs), special education, and intervention specialists. At grade-level meetings, the recommendations of the core team are presented, with the grade-level team having the opportunity to counter the core team's decision. Any alteration to the core team decision must be based on data brought to the team by the grade-level staff. Examination of progress monitoring data for those students currently in Tier 2 or 3, as well as other data collected as part of the process (curriculum-embedded tests such as end-of-level or unit tests), is discussed and decisions on student tier placement are finalized. Implementation fidelity of the interventions is also part of the discussion.

Forms 14 and 15 provide checklists that can be used to determine the steps that core teams and grade-level teams should be following.

GRADE-LEVEL GROUP GOAL SETTING

One of the first responsibilities of the core team is to examine the percentage of students meeting skill benchmarks in each grade at each assessment point and establish what would be reasonable but challenging goals for the grade as a group to reach at the next benchmark level. Achieving the goals requires that strategies be implemented within the core instructional program that will maximize the learning outcomes for all students. Discussion of such strategies, including a mechanism to examine the fidelity with which these strategies are put in place, also is a part of the core team's focus.

Several tools can be used to support the setting of grade-level group goals. To move students who are currently below benchmark to levels at or above benchmark at the next assessment period, one must accelerate the rate of students' performance above the level that typically performing students would advance. In other words, when one looks at the universal screening data, one determines what level of performance attained by a third grader in the fall must be reached in winter if they were to stay at benchmark. For example, when using the benchmarks established by DIBELS 6th Edition (see Table 4), one can see that a third grader in the fall would be reading at 77 WCPM and would need to be at 92 WCPM at winter, 18 weeks later. The rate of improvement (ROI) for this typical student would be 0.8 WCPM/week (92 – 77/18 weeks). For a student below benchmark to "catch up," they would need to move at a rate greater than 0.8 WCPM/week. Based on the work of Fuchs, an ambitious level of change would be somewhere between one and a half and two times the typical rate. We have found that a rate of one and a half times the typical rate works well in setting reasonable yet ambitious group goals. Thus, one would select a rate of 1.2 WCPM/week (0.8 × 1.5 = 1.2) as the targeted ROI for the group. This process can be adapted for use with updated benchmark data and in other skill areas beyond reading.

TABLE 4. DIBELS 6th Edition Benchmarks and Rate of Improvement across Grades across the School Year

Measure	Fall	Winter (fall–winter ROI)	Spring (winter–spring ROI)	Total year ROI
K-ISF	8	25 (0.9)	N/A	
K-PSF	0	18 (1.0)	35 (0.9)	1.0
K-NWF	0	13 (0.7)	25 (0.7)	0.7
1—NWF	24	50 (1.4)	50 (NA)	0.7
1—ORF	0	20 (1.1)	40 (1.1)	1.1
2	44	68 (1.3)	90 (1.2)	1.3
3	77	92 (0.8)	110 (1.0)	0.9
4	93	105 (0.7)	118 (0.7)	0.7
5	104	115 (0.6)	124 (0.5)	0.6

Using Form 16 (instructions for Form 16 are provided on page 158), the core team can set the goals for moving students from strategic support to benchmark in their performance for the next assessment period. The terms *benchmark* and *strategic* are how some assessment suites, such as DIBELS, have referred to levels of risk based on universal screening scores and recommended levels of support. Benchmark refers to levels of achievement consistent with grade-level expectations; students scoring in this range are likely to meet subsequent benchmark targets with core instruction alone. Strategic refers to achievement levels below benchmark, such students are at some risk of not meeting subsequent benchmark targets (i.e., students who would likely benefit from some strategic level of support supplemental to core instruction). *Intensive* has been used to refer to achievement levels representing the most risk and students that are in need of more intensive forms of support in addition to core instruction. Other assessment suites may refer to these types of achievement categories with different terms and may have fewer (or additional) categories. An illustration of the process is provided in Figure 16, based on the data from Figure 17.

- **Step 1.** The DIBELS 6th Edition ROI for moving from fall to winter for students reaching benchmark levels is 0.7 WCPM/week. This value is placed in the box under Step 1.

- **Step 2.** The target ROI is calculated by multiplying the typical ROI by the rate of acceleration—in this case, 1.5—which equals 1.05 or rounded to 1.1 WCPM/week.

- **Step 3.** The expected gain in number of words is calculated by multiplying the targeted ROI by the number of weeks until the next benchmark assessment (usually 18 weeks, half of a school year). In this case, the calculation is $1.1 \times 18 = 19.8$ words, rounded to 20.

- **Step 4.** The benchmark target for the next assessment period is first identified. Using the DIBELS 6th Edition benchmarks in this example, as seen in Table

Tools for MTSS: Data-Based Decision Making

Goal-Setting Worksheet: Strategic to Benchmark

1. Determine the typical rate of improvement (ROI; look at the AIMSweb or DIBELS benchmark sheet).

Typical Rate of Improvement:
0.7

2. Determine target ROI (multiply the typical ROI by 1.5).

0.7	(Typical ROI) × **1.5** (Multiplier) =	1.05	(Target ROI)
0.7	× 1.5 = 1.06	≈ 1.1	

3. Determine expected gain (EG).
   a. Multiply the target ROI (your result from Step 2) by the number of weeks until the next benchmark assessment (typically this is an 18-week period).
   b. This is the number of words you expect the students to gain in the coming benchmark period.

1.1	(Typical ROI) ×	18	(Number of weeks) =	19.8	(EG)
1.1	× 18	= 19.8	≈ 20		

4. Calculate the cutoff score.
   a. Find the benchmark target for the next assessment period.
   b. Subtract your number from Step 3 from the next benchmark target.
   c. This gives you the cutoff score.

104	(Next benchmark target) –	20	(EG) =	84	(Cutoff score)
104	– 20	= 84			

5. Determine how many students you can expect to get to benchmark. Determine how many students at the strategic level are at or above the cutoff number (the number you determined in Step 4).
   a. Look at the distribution.
   b. Find the cutoff score in the graph.
   c. Count how many students are at or above that cutoff score. (Remember to count the number of students who are already at benchmark as well.)

Strategic students at or above cutoff number: _____4_____
Number of students already at benchmark: _____24_____
Total number of students expected to be at benchmark by next assessment: _____28_____

6. Convert the number of students you expect to reach or stay at benchmark in time for the next assessment into a percentage:
   a. Divide the number of students from Step 5 by the total number of students at the grade level and multiply by 100.
   b. This is the percentage of students you expect to reach benchmark in the next assessment . . . your goal!

28	(Total: Step 5) ÷	38	(Total # of students) =	.74	× 100 =	74	%
28	÷ 38	= .74	× 100 =	74	%		
Goal for next assessment:	74	%					

FIGURE 16. Example of data for goal setting in the fall for a fourth-grade class.

4th Grade: Fall 2006

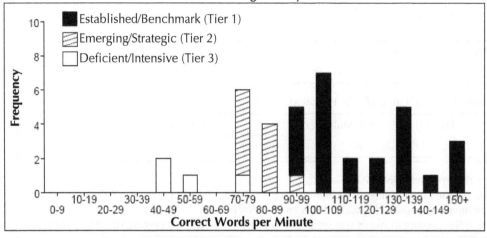

	0-9	10-19	20-29	30-39	40-49	50-59	60-69	70-79	80-89	90-99	100-109	110-119	120-129	130-139	140-149	150+
Deficient	0	0	0	0	2	1	0	1	0	0	0	0	0	0	0	0
Emerging	0	0	0	0	0	0	0	5	4	1	0	0	0	0	0	0
Established	0	0	0	0	0	0	0	0	0	4	7	2	2	5	1	3

	Description	Target Range (WCPM)	Ns	%s
☐	Deficient/Intensive (Tier 3)	<71	4	11%
▨	Emerging/Strategic (Tier 2)	71 – 92	10	26%
■	Established/Benchmark (Tier 1)	93+	24	63%

Goals for next benchmark

	Next Benchmark:	Target Range (WCPM)	Goal: Number of Students	Goal: % of Students
☐	Deficient/Intensive (Tier 3)			
▨	Emerging/Strategic (Tier 2)			
■	Established/Benchmark (Tier 1)			

FIGURE 17. Data from fourth-grade fall DIBELS 6th Edition ORF used for goal setting.

4, the winter benchmark for students in fourth grade is 104 WCPM. This score is subtracted from the expected gain score, resulting in what is called the *cutoff score*. In this case, the cutoff score is 84 (104 – 80). The cutoff score represents the students who, if their rate of performance accelerated between fall and winter at the targeted ROI, would likely reach benchmark at the winter assessment.

• **Step 5.** The number of students within the strategic range but at or above the cutoff score of 84 is determined. Looking at the data displayed in Figure 17, there are a total of 5 students between scores of 80 and 92. If one looked at the exact distribution of the scores between 80 and 89, one would find that 4 of the 5 students would be between 84 and 92. A total of 24 students are currently at benchmark (see

Figure 17), resulting in a total predicted number of students at benchmark by winter of 28.

● **Step 6.** The number of students predicted to be at benchmark is divided by the total number of students in the grade—in this case, 38—resulting in a goal of 74% of students at benchmark by the winter assessment.

MEETING GRADE-LEVEL GOALS

Once the core team identifies the goals for the next benchmark period, team members must discuss strategies and barriers related to reaching these goals. Another tool useful for core team discussion may be found in Form 17. This tool requires teams to record the specific goals for the next benchmark period, identify barriers and concerns that may be evident in meeting the goals, brainstorm solutions to potential barriers, and select the solution that could best resolve barriers and concerns. This simple tool helps team members discuss openly the opportunities and instructional challenges in making sure that goals are met.

DATA DISPLAYS FOR GRADE-LEVEL MEETINGS

Core team members prepare the dataset for examination and interpretation by the grade-level teams. Use of spreadsheets or other forms of data management is essential for efficient discussion at these meetings. Typically, these meetings last from 30 to 45 minutes, during which all students in an entire grade must be discussed. To facilitate the process, data displays need to be simple, easy to understand, and allow quick determination of the impact of the instructional program in place. Although the core team will have carefully examined these data in some detail and made recommendations for student assignment to tiers as well as instructional programs matched to skill needs within those tiers, it is essential that grade-level teams, composed primarily of instructional staff, have an equal level of skill in interpreting these data.

Staff at each MTSS implementation may have a particular data display process that works best for them. The data shown in Figure 18 are a portion of reading data from a winter grade-level team meeting for third-grade students. Microsoft Excel was used as the database, and these data were displayed for staff during the meeting. Presented on the spreadsheet were all the relevant data sources, including scores on students' DIBELS oral reading fluency (both WCPM and percentage of accuracy are displayed), the instructional recommendation made by the DIBELS program, scores on a reading maze measure, scores on a group-administered measure of reading comprehension called 4sight benchmark assessment, and the current attained ROI from progress monitoring data for those students at Tier 2 or 3. Both fall and winter scores are displayed along with the core team recommendations. Finally, the data are color-coded (shown in shades of gray) to easily see when a student's score is below benchmark (light gray) or in the at-risk range (dark gray). The data are

			Fall 07							Winter 08					
				ORF Acc. > 95%			4Sight Prof ≥ 70% Basic = 54–69%				ORF Acc. > 95%			4Sight Prof ≥ 70% Basic = 54–69%	
Last	First	Teacher	ORF (77)		IR	MAZE (12)		Group	PM ROI	ORF (92)		IR	Maze (13)		Decision
Students in benchmark in fall															
S	M	Z	149	98.7	B	23	77%	B	NA	171	99.4	B	28	90%	Stay
E	V	Z	148	99.3	B	22	83%	B	NA	164	99.4	B	20	80%	Stay
Se	J	W	142	98.6	B	21	77%	B	NA	154	100	B	21	90%	Stay
C	A	Z	140	100	B	19	80%	B (gr4)	NA	142	98.6	B	20	83%	Stay
K	T	Z	134	100	B	20	63%	B	NA	133	99.3	B	26	77%	Stay
L	J	L	127	98.4	B	21	70%	B	NA	119	98.3	B	8	70%	Stay
Vo	K	L	112	97.3	B			B	NA	117	98.1	B	12	50%	Move to low benchmark?
Pi	J	W	108		B	12	63%	B	NA	128	100	B	19	87%	Stay
Po	D	W	106	98.1	B	21	73%	B	NA	145	100	B	23	83%	Stay
G	B	L	92	98.9	B	15	63%	B	NA	87	98.9	S	15	60%	Move to low benchmark?
D	A	W	66	97.1	S	13	80%	B	1.5	91	98.9	S	15	70%	Move to strategic?
Students in strategic in fall															
C	T	L	88	88	B	14	73%	S-PALS	0.2	83	95.4	S	15	67%	Comprehension needs
J	F	L	72	96	S	13	73%	S-PALS	–0	87	97.8	S	15	83%	Stay
P	G	W	72	98.6	S	9	63%	S-PALS	2.2	75	96.2	S	14	67%	Comprehension needs
J	B	W	62	96.9	S	6	57%	S-PALS	2.1	99	98	B	13	70%	Move to benchmark
S	C	Z	58	78.4	S	16	43%	S-PALS	–1	65	95.6	I	14	43%	Stay—fluency needs
F	C	Z	23	100	I	4	23%	S-PALS	0.3	55	98.2	I	6	40%	Stay—slow but accurate reader
Students in intensive in fall															
T	W	L	51	94.4	I	10	43%	I-CR B1	0.7	56	94.9	I	10	70%	Stay
To	F	Z	47	95.9	I	6	27%	I-CR A	2.3	66	91.7	I	12	70%	Move CR B1
He	J	W	45		I		0%	I-CR B1	0	54	90	I	5	50%	Move down to CR A
G	C	L	35	87.5	I	5	43%	I-CR A	0.3	33	89.2	I	5	17%	Stay
Average			79.2	94.7		13.0	0.6		0.9	93.7	95.9		13.4	70%	

% Prof = 67%

FIGURE 18. Example of a spreadsheet for a grade-level team meeting of third-grade staff. IR, instructional recommendation; PM ROI, progress monitoring rate of improvement; B, benchmark; S, strategic; I, intensive; PALS, peer-assisted learning strategies; CR, corrective reading.

also divided into those students who were assigned to benchmark, strategic (Tier 2), or intensive (Tier 3) groups based on their fall assessment data. Also indicated on the data display is the specific instructional group to which the student is assigned. In this particular MTSS implementation, students at Tier 2 received PALS (peer-assisted learning strategies; *kc.vanderbilt.edu/pals*) at two levels with targets for different reading skills, and students at Tier 3 received different levels of the SRA Corrective Reading Program.

Looking down the last column of Figure 18, one can see that the team decisions included changing instructional levels within tiers (Vo was moved to low-benchmark group; C in strategic has an emphasis on comprehension), as well as moving students between tiers (J in strategic was moved to benchmark, given his improvement in scores).

TOOLS FOR INDIVIDUAL STUDENT DECISIONS

At both core and grade-level team meetings, the progress monitoring of those students currently in tiered interventions is examined. Progress monitoring data contribute valuable information to these meetings in helping to ensure that students are being supported and intervention resources are being used effectively. There may be a number of students with progress monitoring data; therefore, teams need to efficiently determine if the data support continuing the student in the current level and type of support, making an instructional change, or raising a goal. Form 18 can be a useful tool to facilitate these decisions in an efficient and organized way. Each student's name and current level of intervention support are recorded for each student, the team examined the progress monitoring data and collaboratively makes a determination, and includes a justification for their decision. Decision-making skills used in Exercise 13 earlier in this chapter and in Chapter 7 of *Academic Skills Problems, Fifth Edition* would be used here.

EXERCISE IN DATA-BASED DECISION MAKING

Figure 19 presents an opportunity to practice data-based decision making using data from universal screening and progress monitoring (when applicable). Data are presented following the fourth-grade winter benchmarking period of a hypothetical classroom. The available data sources for students who were at benchmark at the fall of the school year are the outcomes of the fall and winter D-ORF scores, an indication of whether students achieved the DIBELS 6th Edition benchmark (105 WCPM) for winter, the accuracy of students' performance on the D-ORF (95% or better is expected), and students' percentage correct on the 4sight benchmark assessments (a group-administered measure of reading vocabulary and comprehension) taken at baseline (beginning of school year) and midyear. A score of 57% on this measure represents proficiency. For students assigned to strategic or intensive groups, an indication of the degree to which they achieved the benchmark score of 105 WCPM, as well as whether they achieved the score marking the strategic level (between 83 and 104 WCPM), was noted. In addition, data from students' progress

Students at Benchmark at Fall of Year

	Fall DORF Score	Winter DORF Score	Reached Winter Bnchmk Target of 105*	Reached Winter Strtgc Target of 83	Winter DORF Accuracy (95%)	4Sight Test 1; 57% = P Total	4Sight Test 3; 57% = P Total	Progress Monitoring Targeted ROI	Progress Monitoring Attained ROI	Decision
Locke, John	128	134	✓		96%	77%	80%			
Shephard, Jack	102	118	✓		95%	53%	57%			
Kwon, Jin-Soo	142	147	✓		97%	70%	73%			
Austen, Kate	103	148	✓		98%	70%	80%			
Reyes, Hugo	133	142	✓		99%	53%	70%			
Littlejohn, Claire	113	140			100%	40%	50%			
Jarrah, Sayid	93	99			96%	42%	44%			

Students at Strategic at Fall of Year

	Fall DORF Score	Winter DORF Score	Reached Winter Bnchmk Target of 105*	Reached Winter Strtgc Target of 83	Winter DORF Accuracy (95%)	4Sight Test 1; 57% = P Total	4Sight Test 3; 57% = P Total	Progress Monitoring Targeted ROI 0.7 = Exp ROI	Progress Monitoring Attained ROI	Decision
Flowers, May	92	106	✓		96%	60%	63%	1.64	2.28	
Showers, April	83	110	✓		94%	73%	67%	1.14	1.56	
Wanka, Willy	75	91		◄	94%	43%	53%	1.14	2.88	
Sam Spade	67	99		◄	93%	43%	67%	1.00	2.01	
Flinstone, Wilma	71	91		◄	98%	67%	70%	1.78	1.85	
Rubble, Barney	73	90			93%	60%	47%	1.00	2.47	

Students at Intensive at Fall of Year

	Fall DORF Score	Winter DORF Score	Reached Winter Bnchmk Target of 105*	Reached Winter Strtgc Target of 83	Winter DORF Accuracy (95%)	4Sight Test 1; 57% = P Total	4Sight Test 3; 57% = P Total	Progress Monitoring Targeted ROI 0.7 = Exp ROI	Progress Monitoring Attained ROI	Decision
Rubble, Betty	51	62			98%	10%	23%	2.47	1.53	
Bush, Rose	43	58			95%	37%	57%	3.60	-0.15	
Lincoln, Abraham	41	60			92%	33%	37%	0.82	1.64	
Bugg, June	49	56			89%	47%	37%	2.20	1.32	
March, Ides	56	92		◄	97%	73%	80%	1.08	4.14	

FIGURE 19. Data for practice in data-based decision making.

monitoring are provided. The target ROI for each student is provided—that is, the ROI needed for the student to reach the established benchmark goal along with the student's attained ROI throughout the period in which they received tiered intervention. Note that the expected or typical ROI for students, based on fall-to-winter benchmarks for the time period, was 0.7 WCPM/week.

Readers are asked to examine those students whose names are highlighted in gray and to write your decision as to whether each should remain within the tier where they are currently assigned, whether their goals should be increased, or whether a change should be made. To assist readers further, Figures 20 and 21 provide the actual progress monitoring for each student. An answer key is provided in Figures 22 and 23, where a fuller explanation of the rationale behind the decisions is offered.

May Lynn Flowers

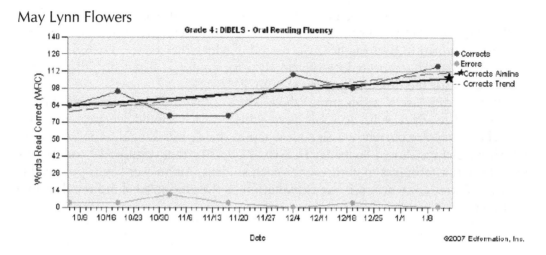

April Lynn Showers

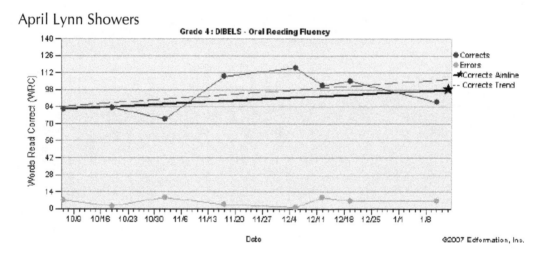

Sam Spade

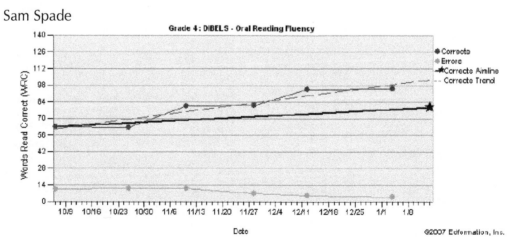

FIGURE 20. Progress monitoring graphs for three fourth-grade students receiving strategic levels of support in the fall of the year.

Abraham Lincoln

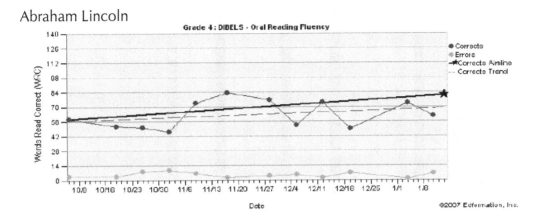

June Bugg

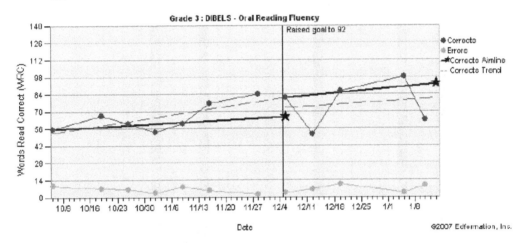

March Ides

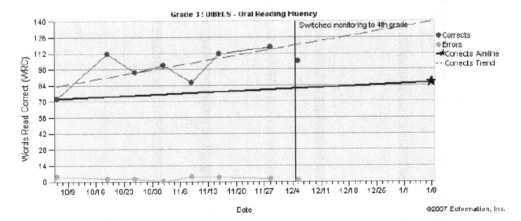

FIGURE 21. Progress monitoring graphs for three fourth-grade students receiving intensive levels of support in the fall of the year.

Students at Benchmark at Fall of Year	Fall DORF Score	Winter DORF Score	Reached Winter Bnchmk Target of 105'	Reached Winter Strtgc Target of 83	Winter DORF Accuracy (95%)	4Sight Test 1; 57% = P Total	4Sight Test 3; 57% = P Total	Progress Monitoring Targeted ROI	Progress Monitoring Attained ROI	Decision
Locke, John	128	134	✓		96%	77%	80%			
Shephard, Jack	102	118	✓		95%	53%	57%			Continue—on watch—4sight
Kwon, Jin-Soo	142	147	✓		97%	70%	73%			
Austen, Kate	103	148	✓		98%	70%	80%			
Reyes, Hugo	133	142	✓		99%	53%	70%			Continue
Littlejohn, Claire	113	140	✓		100%	40%	50%			
Jarrah, Sayid	93	99			96%	42%	44%			Tier 2 vocab & comp—4sight

Students at Strategic at Fall of Year	Fall DORF Score	Winter DORF Score	Reached Winter Bnchmk Target of 105'	Reached Winter Strtgc Target of 83	Winter DORF Accuracy (95%)	4Sight Test 1; 57% = P Total	4Sight Test 3; 57% = P Total	Progress Monitoring Targeted ROI 0.7 = Exp ROI	Progress Monitoring Attained ROI	Decision
Flowers, May	92	106	✓		96%	60%	63%	1.64	2.28	Exit to Tier 1—PM & 4sight
Showers, April	83	110	✓		94%	73%	67%	1.14	1.56	Exit to Tier 1—PM & 4sight
Wanka, Willy	75	91		◄	94%	43%	53%	1.14	2.88	
Sam Spade	67	99		◄	93%	43%	67%	1.00	2.01	Continue - raise goal
Flinstone, Wilma	71	91		◄	98%	67%	70%	1.78	1.85	
Rubble, Barney	73	90		◄	93%	60%	47%	1.00	2.47	

Students at Intensive at Fall of Year	Fall DORF Score	Winter DORF Score	Reached Winter Bnchmk Target of 105'	Reached Winter Strtgc Target of 83	Winter DORF Accuracy (95%)	4Sight Test 1; 57% = P Total	4Sight Test 3; 57% = P Total	Progress Monitoring Targeted ROI 0.7 = Exp ROI	Progress Monitoring Attained ROI	Decision
Rubble, Betty	51	62			98%	10%	23%	2.47	1.53	
Bush, Rose	43	58			95%	37%	57%	3.60	-0.15	
Lincoln, Abraham	41	60			92%	33%	37%	0.82	1.64	Continue—change in instructional program—comp and fluency
Bugg, June	49	56			89%	47%	37%	2.20	1.32	Continue—change in instructional program—comp and fluency
March, Ides	56	92		◄	97%	73%	80%	1.08	4.14	Exit to Tier 2- Increase in ORF, PM, 4sight

FIGURE 22. Answer key for practice in data-based decision making.

Student	Current Tier	Decision	Rationale
Shephard, Jack	1	Continue—on watch—4sight	Well above benchmark in ORF; accuracy is acceptable; 4sight is barely proficient, suggesting some potential struggles in comprehension; on watch with emphasis on comprehension strategies
Reyes, Hugo	1	Continue	Well above benchmark in ORF; highly accurate; 4sight is well above proficient level
Jarrah, Sayid	1	Tier 2	Below ORF benchmark; small gain from fall to winter in ORF; reads accurately, but 4sight is below proficient. Place into instructional group focused on vocabulary building and comprehension
Flowers, May	2	Exit to Tier 1	Reached winter ORF benchmark, maintained accuracy, attained ROI > target ROI; PM graph supports consistent performance; achieved proficiency on 4sight
Showers, April	2	Exit to Tier 1	Reached winter ORF benchmark; accuracy just slightly below expectation; attained ROI > targeted ROI; graph suggests trend that is at or above goal, although slight decline noted on last data point; 4sight remain at proficient
Spade, Sam	2	Continue—raise goal	Did not reach winter ORF benchmark; large increase from fall to winter ORF; accuracy <95%; attained ROI > target ROI; PM above target
Lincoln, Abraham	3	Continue—change in instructional program—comp and fluency	Did not reach strategic winter ORF benchmark; accuracy <95%, attained ROI < target ROI, but attained ROI > expected ROI; 4sight very much below proficient. Emphasis in instructional program needs to shift to work specifically in fluency building and comprehension
Bugg, June	3	Continue—change in instructional program—comp and fluency	Did not reach strategic winter ORF; very small gain fall to winter in ORF; accuracy substantially <95%; PM had been below grade level; attained ROI < target ROI after goal was raised to 92; 4sight very much below proficient. Emphasis in instructional program needs to shift to work specifically in fluency building and comprehension
March, Ides	3	Exit to Tier 2	Reached strategic winter ORF benchmark; accuracy >95%; attained ROI > targeted ROI; PM shows ability to succeed at fourth-grade level; 4sight is proficient

FIGURE 23. Rationale for decisions related to tier assignment by team.

Level of Implementation Scale—Core Data Team

Data Analysis	Not Relevant	Not Evident (0 pt)	Partially Evident (1 pt)	Fully Evident (2 pt)
1. Student data are prepared for the meeting in a teacher-friendly format and sent to teachers in advance. The principal decides who is to be the session facilitator and arranges the meeting logistics. *Facilitator:*				
2. Attendees include principal, all data team members, as well as others. *Designated attendees:*				
3. Data team sets measurable goals for each grade level, presented in terms of specific percentages of students reaching proficiency on screening assessments (a specific number is stated for each goal, e.g., "Right now we have 70% of our first graders at benchmark on the DIBELS Word Reading Fluency test. By January, 80% of first-grade students will be at benchmark"). *Specific goals:*				
4. Data team identifies barriers to meeting goals by designated time and addresses all concerns.				
5. Data team brainstorms ideas to address concerns. Strategies are discussed and those that are most beneficial/feasible to implement are identified.				
6. Data team plans the logistics of implementing agreed-upon strategies in all classrooms in that grade level (at least one specific strategy is discussed for scheduling, intervention implementation, and/or sharing progress monitoring data). *Strategy discussed:*				
7. Data team schedules a time to review the progress of students in follow-up meetings to determine the efficacy of implemented strategies (a specific time and date are set for the follow-up meeting). *Follow-up meeting date/time:*				
8. Data team discusses how to monitor the fidelity of the intervention (at least one strategy is discussed). *Strategy discussed:*				
9. Data team monitors the student's progress.				
10. Data team fine-tunes the strategies.				
TOTAL = ____ / ____ : ____ **% Implementation**				

From *Academic Skills Problems Fifth Edition Workbook* by Edward S. Shapiro and Nathan H. Clemens. Copyright © 2023 The Guilford Press. Permission to photocopy this form is granted to purchasers of this book for personal use or use with students (see copyright page for details). Purchasers can download additional copies of this form (see the box at the end of the table of contents).

FORM 15

Level of Implementation Scale—Grade-Level Data Team

Data Analysis	Not Relevant	Not Evident (0 pt)	Partially Evident (1 pt)	Fully Evident (2 pt)
1. Student data are prepared for the meeting by the classroom teacher and brought to the meeting. A DDMT member acts as facilitator of meeting. *Facilitator:*				
2. Attendees include principal, all teachers from the grade level, and data manager(s) as well as others. *Designated attendees:*				
3. Data team reviews measurable goals set by core team for each grade level, presented in terms of specific percentages of students reaching proficiency on screening assessments (a specific number is stated for each goal, e.g., *"Right now we have 70% of our first graders at benchmark on the DIBELS Word Reading Fluency test. By January, 80% of first-grade students will be at benchmark").* *Specific goals:*				
4. Data team discusses strategies identified by core team to be implemented across all classes.				
5. Grade-level team briefly reviews progress monitoring data to evaluate performance of individual students in terms of which students are above, below, or at target. Based on this evaluation, the team decides which students are in need of instructional or goal changes.				
6. Grade-level team reviews performance of those students identified as in need of a goal or instructional change to determine appropriate action. Decisions regarding changes should be made as a group.				
7. Grade-level teams identify students in need of more support at Tier 2 or Tier 3. *The grade-level teams identify students that will need more frequent assessment. These students include the students with the most significant difficulties and "stalled" students.*				
8. Grade-level teams discuss how to monitor the fidelity of the intervention (at least one strategy is discussed). *Strategy discussed:*				
9. Grade-level teams fine-tune any strategies being used for Tier 2 and Tier 3 interventions.				
10. Grade-level teams schedule a time to review the progress of students in follow-up meetings to determine the efficacy of implemented changes (a specific time and date are set for the follow-up meeting). *Follow-up meeting date/time:*				
TOTAL = _____ / _____ : _____ **% Implementation**				

Academic Skills Problems Fifth Edition Workbook by Edward S. Shapiro and Nathan H. Clemens. Copyright © 2023 The Guilford Press. Permission to photocopy this form is granted to purchasers of this book for personal use or use with students (see copyright page for details). Purchasers can download additional copies of this form (see the box at the end of the table of contents).

INSTRUCTIONS FOR GOAL-SETTING WORKSHEET: STRATEGIC TO BENCHMARK

1. Determine the **typical rate of improvement** (**ROI**; look at the AIMSweb or DIBELS Benchmark sheet).

2. Determine **target ROI** (multiply the typical ROI by 1.5).

3. Determine **expected gain** (**EG**).
   a. Multiply the target ROI (your result from Step 2) by the number of weeks till the next benchmark assessment (typically this is an 18-week period).
   b. This is the number of words you expect the students to gain in the coming benchmark period.

4. Calculate the **cutoff score**.
   a. Find the benchmark target for the next assessment period.
   b. Subtract your number from Step 3 from the next benchmark target.
   c. This gives you the cutoff score.

5. **Determine how many students you can expect to get to benchmark**. Determine how many students at the strategic level are at or above the cutoff number (the number you determined in Step 4).
   a. Look at the distribution scores.
   b. Find the cutoff score in the distribution.
   c. Count how many students are at or above that cutoff score. (Remember to count the number of students who are already at benchmark as well.)

6. Convert the number of students you expect to reach or stay at benchmark in time for the next assessment into a **percentage**:
   a. Divide the number of students from Step 5 by the total number of students at the grade level and multiply by 100.
   b. This is the percentage of students you expect to reach benchmark in the next assessment . . . your goal!

FORM 16

Goal-Setting Worksheet: Strategic to Benchmark

1. Determine the typical rate of improvement (ROI; look at the AIMSweb or DIBELS benchmark sheet).

Typical Rate of Improvement:

2. Determine target ROI (multiply the typical ROI by 1.5).

_____ (Typical ROI) × **1.5** (Multiplier) = _____ (Target ROI)

_____ × _____ = _____

3. Determine expected gain (EG).
   a. Multiply the target ROI (your result from Step 2) by the number of weeks until the next benchmark assessment (typically this is an 18-week period).
   b. This is the number of words you expect the students to gain in the coming benchmark period.

_____ (Typical ROI) × _____ (Number of weeks) = _____ (EG)

_____ × _____ = _____

4. Calculate the cutoff score.
   a. Find the benchmark target for the next assessment period.
   b. Subtract your number from Step 3 from the next benchmark target.
   c. This gives you the cutoff score.

_____ (Next benchmark target) − _____ (EG) = _____ (Cutoff score)

_____ − _____ = _____

(continued)

From *Academic Skills Problems Fifth Edition Workbook* by Edward S. Shapiro and Nathan H. Clemens. Copyright © 2023 The Guilford Press. Permission to photocopy this form is granted to purchasers of this book for personal use or use with students (see copyright page for details). Purchasers can download additional copies of this form (see the box at the end of the table of contents).

5. Determine how many students you can expect to get to benchmark. Determine how many students at the strategic level are at or above the cutoff number (the number you determined in Step 4).
   a. Look at the distribution.
   b. Find the cutoff score in the graph.
   c. Count how many students are at or above that cutoff score. (Remember to count the number of students who are already at benchmark as well.)

Strategic students at or above cutoff number: _____

Number of students already at benchmark: _____

Total number of students expected to be at benchmark by next assessment: _____

6. Convert the number of students you expect to reach or stay at benchmark in time for the next assessment into a percentage:
   a. Divide the number of students from Step 5 by the total number of students at the grade level and multiply by 100.
   b. This is the percentage of students you expect to reach benchmark in the next assessment . . . your goal!

_____ (Total: Step 5) ÷ _____ (Total # of students) = _____ × 100 = _____ %

_____ ÷ _____ = _____ × 100 = _____ %

Goal for next assessment: _____ %

FORM 17

Grade-Level Goal Review, Barriers, and Solutions

1. **Goals:** Goals for the next benchmark period, as determined by the data decision team (using typical rates of improvement multiplied by approximately 1.5)

Grade 2   Measure: ORF

	Current Status		Next Benchmark Goal	
Circle Current: **Fall or Spring**	**Number of Students**	**%**	**Number of Students**	**%**
Deficient/Intensive (Tier 3)				
Emerging/Strategic (Tier 2)				
Established/Benchmark (Tier 1)				

2. **Barriers and Concerns:** What barriers do you foresee in attaining these goals? What concerns do you have?

3. **Brainstorm:** Brainstorm strategies, supports, materials, training, or services needed to achieve goal(s) for 5–10 minutes. List all suggestions below.

4. Analyze each suggestion above. Consider those that are evidence-based, practical, and feasible within the given time frame. Circle those that meet these criteria.

From *Academic Skills Problems Fifth Edition Workbook* by Edward S. Shapiro and Nathan H. Clemens. Copyright © 2023 The Guilford Press. Permission to photocopy this form is granted to purchasers of this book for personal use or use with students (see copyright page for details). Purchasers can download additional copies of this form (see the box at the end of the table of contents).

Grade-Level Meeting Progress Monitoring Data-Based Decision-Making Form

Student	Tier	Progress	Decision	Comment
	☐ Strategic ☐ Intensive	☐ Above Target ☐ Near Target ☐ Below Target	☐ Continue ☐ Raise Goal ☐ Instructional Change/Modification	
	☐ Strategic ☐ Intensive	☐ Above Target ☐ Near Target ☐ Below Target	☐ Continue ☐ Raise Goal ☐ Instructional Change/Modification	
	☐ Strategic ☐ Intensive	☐ Above Target ☐ Near Target ☐ Below Target	☐ Continue ☐ Raise Goal ☐ Instructional Change/Modification	
	☐ Strategic ☐ Intensive	☐ Above Target ☐ Near Target ☐ Below Target	☐ Continue ☐ Raise Goal ☐ Instructional Change/Modification	
	☐ Strategic ☐ Intensive	☐ Above Target ☐ Near Target ☐ Below Target	☐ Continue ☐ Raise Goal ☐ Instructional Change/Modification	
	☐ Strategic ☐ Intensive	☐ Above Target ☐ Near Target ☐ Below Target	☐ Continue ☐ Raise Goal ☐ Instructional Change/Modification	
	☐ Strategic ☐ Intensive	☐ Above Target ☐ Near Target ☐ Below Target	☐ Continue ☐ Raise Goal ☐ Instructional Change/Modification	
	☐ Strategic ☐ Intensive	☐ Above Target ☐ Near Target ☐ Below Target	☐ Continue ☐ Raise Goal ☐ Instructional Change/Modification	
	☐ Strategic ☐ Intensive	☐ Above Target ☐ Near Target ☐ Below Target	☐ Continue ☐ Raise Goal ☐ Instructional Change/Modification	
	☐ Strategic ☐ Intensive	☐ Above Target ☐ Near Target ☐ Below Target	☐ Continue ☐ Raise Goal ☐ Instructional Change/Modification	
	☐ Strategic ☐ Intensive	☐ Above Target ☐ Near Target ☐ Below Target	☐ Continue ☐ Raise Goal ☐ Instructional Change/Modification	
	☐ Strategic ☐ Intensive	☐ Above Target ☐ Near Target ☐ Below Target	☐ Continue ☐ Raise Goal ☐ Instructional Change/Modification	
	☐ Strategic ☐ Intensive	☐ Above Target ☐ Near Target ☐ Below Target	☐ Continue ☐ Raise Goal ☐ Instructional Change/Modification	

Academic Skills Problems Fifth Edition Workbook by Edward S. Shapiro and Nathan H. Clemens. Copyright © 2023 The Guilford Press. Permission to photocopy this form is granted to purchasers of this book for personal use or use with students (see copyright page for details). Purchasers can download additional copies of this form (see the box at the end of the table of contents).

References

Brown-Chidsey, R., Bronaugh, L., & McGraw, K. (2009). *RTI in the classroom: Guidelines and recipes for success.* New York: Guilford Press.

Brown-Chidsey, R., & Steege, M. W. (2010). *Response to intervention: Principles and strategies for effective practice* (2nd ed.). New York: Guilford Press.

Erion, J., Davenport, C., Rodax, N., Scholl, B., & Hardy, J. (2009). Cover–copy–compare and spelling: One versus three repetitions. *Journal of Behavioral Education, 18,* 319–330.

Fuchs, L. S. (2003). Assessing intervention responsiveness: Conceptual and technical issues. *Learning Disabilities Research and Practice, 18,* 172–186.

Fuchs, L. S., Hamlett, C. L., & Fuchs, D. (1999). *Monitoring basic skills progress: Basic math concepts and applications—blackline masters.* Austin, TX: PRO-ED.

Gickling, E. E., & Havertape, S. (1981). *Curriculum-based assessment (CBA).* Minneapolis, MN: School Psychology Inservice Training Network.

Gresham, F. M. (2002). Responsiveness to intervention: An alternative approach to the identification of learning disabilities. In R. Bradley, L. Danielson, & D. P. Hallahan (Eds.), *Identification of learning disabilities: Research to practice* (pp. 467–519). Mahwah, NJ: Erlbaum.

Hasbrouck, J., & Tindal, G. (2017). *An update to compiled ORF norms.* Eugene: University of Oregon, Behavioral Research & Teaching. Retrieved from *www.brtprojects.org/wp-content/uploads/2017/10/TechRpt_1702ORFNorms_Fini.pdf.*

Marston, D., Muyskens, P., Lau, M. Y., & Canter, A. (2003). Problem-solving model for decision making with high-incidence disabilities: The Minneapolis experience. *Learning Disabilities Research and Practice, 18,* 187–200.

National Association of State Directors of Special Education. (2006). *Response to intervention: Policy considerations and implementation.* Washington, DC: Author.

Rathvon, N. (2008). *Effective school interventions: Strategies for enhancing academic achievement and social competence* (2nd ed.). New York: Guilford Press.

Shapiro, E. S. (1990). An integrated model for curriculum-based assessment. *School Psychology Review, 19,* 331–349.

Shapiro, E. S., Hilt-Panahon, A., & Gischlar, K. L. (2010). Implementing proven research in school-based practices: Progress monitoring within a response-to-intervention model. In M. R. Shinn & H. M. Walker (Eds.), *Interventions for achievement and behavior problems in a three-tier model including RTI* (pp. 175–192). Washington, DC: National Association of School Psychologists.

Shapiro, E. S., Zigmond, N., Wallace, T., & Marston, D. (Eds.). (2011). *Models for implementing response-to-intervention: Tools, outcomes, and implications.* New York: Guilford Press.

Shinn, M. R. (1988). Development of curriculum-based local norms for use in special education decision-making. *School Psychology Review, 17,* 61–80.

Shinn, M. R. (1989). *Curriculum-based measurement: Assessing special children.* New York: Guilford Press.

Shinn, M. R., & Walker, H. M. (Eds.). (2010). *Interventions for achievement and behavior problems in a three-tier model including RTI.* Washington, DC: National Association of School Psychologists.

Skinner, C. H., Belifore, P. J., & Pearce, N. (1992). Cover, copy, and compare: Increasing geography accuracy in students with behavior disorders. *School Psychology Review, 21,* 73–81.

Skinner, C. H., Turco, T. L., Beatty, K. L., & Rasavage, C. (1989). Cover, copy, and compare: A method for increasing multiplication performance. *School Psychology Review, 18,* 412–420.

Smith, T. J., Ditmer, K. I., & Skinner, C. H. (2002). Enhancing science performance in students with learning disabilities using cover, copy, compare: A student shows the way. *Psychology in the Schools, 39,* 417–426.

Troia, G. A. (2018, August). *Relations between teacher pedagogical content knowledge and student writing outcomes.* Paper presented at the Biennial Meeting of the Special Interest Group on Writing of the European Association for Research on Learning and Instruction, Antwerp, Belgium.

Vaughn, S., Linan-Thompson, S., & Hickman, P. (2003). Response to instruction as a means of identifying students with reading/learning disabilities. *Exceptional Children, 69,* 391–409.

Vaughn, S., Wanzek, J., Woodruff, A. L., & Linan-Thompson, S. (2007). Prevention and early identification of students with reading disabilities. In D. Haager, J. Klingner, & S. Vaughn (Eds.), *Evidence-based reading practices for response to intervention* (pp. 11–27). Baltimore: Brookes.